Dedicated to all the great women
who bared it all in contributing
their private moments to this book.

Also Coming Soon:

Baring It All,
the audio book!
...The ultimate way
to generate hot
passion between
yourself and your
lover!

Stay in touch with the latest from Mystic Ridge Books! Bookmark our web site, and surf it every month for our exciting new books and products:

www.mysticridgebooks.com

We're all about the body, mind and soul. And we've got a lot of special books coming your way!

That's Mystic Ridge Books.

To get on our mailing list: photocopy, fill out and send the form below to: Mystic Ridge Books, P.O. Box 66930, Albuquerque, NM 87193.

Name: _____

Address: _____

_____

Email: _____

Kind of books you like: _____

_____

Baring It All

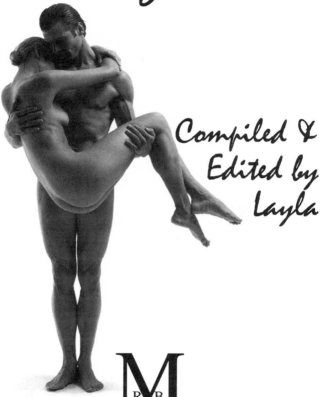

Compiled &
Edited by
Layla

M
R B

MYSTIC RIDGE BOOKS

ALBUQUERQUE, NEW MEXICO

Baring It All

MYSTIC RIDGE BOOKS
P.O. BOX 66930
ALBUQUERQUE, NM 87193-6930
(505) 899-2121
Find us on the World Wide Web at: **www.mysticridgebooks.com**
MYSTIC RIDGE BOOKS is a division of:
Mystic Ridge Productions, Inc.

First Edition, First Printing: November 2003

Copyright © 2003

Library of Congress Catalog Card No.: Pending

ISBN: 0-9672182-8-4

PRINTED & BOUND IN THE UNITED STATES OF AMERICA.

Contents

Foreplay: About This Book

This fabulous book is great for singles, but, unlike many other such books, it's also great for lovers and those who don't normally read erotica. Because, it about the *love* in love-making.

It's a minor miracle that this book ever came to pass. First, we had to find everyday women who have truly experienced great love-making (we turned down some stories that we felt didn't fit that category).

Then we had to convince them to put down on paper the most intimate secrets of their lives, in shocking detail.

With that in mind, you'll realize what a *gift* this book is.

Here is your look into the private lives of

others, of women who have experienced great love-making, and seen their lives enriched and improved by it. Here are openly frank stories, as one contributor put it, "colored by *love* and *romance*."

It's naughty but nice. It's loving but incredibly *sexy*. It's titillating and sexually exciting, yes, but also inspiring, and a sourcebook of ideas that will enhance your love life for many years to come.

Puritans won't like this book; but it's not for them. It's for people who understand the importance of growing as a lover and the benefit of reading about what it *takes* in order to become a *great* lover. The descriptions of events in *Baring It All* aren't nasty; those who are mature enough to accept and celebrate sex as a normal, healthy part of adult life and who hunger for sexual understanding will see the colorful descriptions of sexual events as simply words that convey the visuals we need for these invaluable stories to come to life.

Such tender details are rarely shared. The actual goings-on during sex are never discussed. We are not taught love-making as an *art;* nor are we informed that it is a pursuit that requires *studying* to perfect. So how do we become great lovers?

In this book we offer you role models, blazing the path toward the highest kind of love...an almost indescribable love that few will even come close to attaining...which can only be attained through the most selfless, most spiritual kind of union, which reaches the heights of an almost *religious* experience...an exalted, rapturous experience that unites not just bodies, but spirits...the kind that solidifies relationships and bonds between a man and woman for a lifetime...a union achieved through passionate love-making that lasts for hours, the lovers never wanting it to end.

This book fills a need in today's society, which cannot seem to educate itself about matters that are most important – how to bring your partner and your relationship to that high place, only attainable through the art of great love-making.

Who teaches this? We spend hours and hours, and millions of dollars, learning computer programs, work-related skills, hobby-related skills, and so on, but very very few ever consider the fact that what should be the most important element of our lives – our love lives – requires a learning process, too, and that there are many *levels* to it. Most, unfortunately, never rise above its lowest levels.

The women in this book have climbed up the ladder of love's many steps and have seen the light; they've climbed Love's Mount Everest, having been students of love-making, aware of what it takes. In their stories, we can relive their revelations and learn their secrets, in the hope that we, too, someday, might join them in that rarified club of Enlightened, fully sensitized Lovers, soaring above the rest. *That is the spirit in which these experiences have been shared.*

These stories are about how two can become one, united in true love. It is not flesh of which these writers speak, but of a melting of the flesh and the soaring of souls someplace high above, melded together in exaltation. Nothing, in human terms, is greater than that.

If you haven't yet experienced such a nirvana, then these stories might pave the way. These are the documentation of the best of what is going on behind closed doors, a human endeavor all too often not discussed.

This should not be a taboo subject; if others are to experience this joy, they must have books like this available, so that they know that love-making is more than fucking, or just a physical act -- that's what it is only in its basest form.

What you'll read about here is steamy stuff, yes, but it is also what we've all dreamed about. Love-making with *love* behind it. Love-making motivated by the need to express something so deep and indescribable that only a physical, wordless expression of it is possible.

The stories in this book are meant to be shared and savored with your lover. No matter where you stand in the pantheon of lovers, these stories, when read to your lover, will enhance what you already have and bring you closer together.

Here are the fireworks that are missing from so many of our lives. Here is the road to sexual and spiritual Rapture.

Here are the lessons you need for those great dances in between the sheets (and in a cave, on the kitchen table, over the living room sofa, in the bath, in the shower, etc.).

In this impersonal world, here are the lovers who have broken through the boundaries of humdrum human existence and soared into the heavens, exploding above us in brilliant colors and light so that we can all marvel at what they have achieved.

Now, as some of you might have surmised, many of these stories have been polished from their original forms. You would not have been able to plow through some of what was originally presented to us. They were written by non-writers, and so the first drafts were often crude.

However, Mystic Ridge Books' editors and writers worked closely with the authors, interviewing them in detail, in order to flesh out the stories and make them express what the authors intended. The new drafts were then given to the authors for their OK. We made very sure that every word in this book presented exactly what happened during these incredible events. When the authors signed off on the final versions, they assured us that every emotion, every physical change, every sound, every sensation that they'd experienced was captured in words.

What you hold in your hands, therefore, is an incredibly special and unique documentation of our times, of the best our generation has to offer, in the way of loving ourselves. Don't be surprised if you find these stories so intense that you can only read one or two at a time.

D.C.'s Story: Please Me Up & Down

My man has always been very giving in bed, but what he did to me the other night was absolutely incredible!

Before I tell you about that, though, I need to

provide you with a little background information.

Craig has taught me what real *love-making* is all about. Not sex or fucking, but *love-making*.

There's a big difference, but I don't think I appreciated the distinction until Craig came into my life. Once you've had true *love-making*, you won't want anything less, ever again.

Craig likes to say that *love-making* is a form of nonverbal *communication*.

"Every touch should be worth a thousand words," he told me. "Love-making is a physical expression of passion, of affection, of love, of how you feel toward your lover. The more intense your feelings, the better the Love-making.

"That's what makes Love-making that much more affecting, enjoyable, powerful, meaningful and worthwhile than ordinary sex; but, sadly, most people don't get it."

And, if you think about it, that makes total sense.

Love-making versus fucking to me is all in the way it *feels*. When Craig makes love to me, he's not moving by rote or according to some manual, without purpose; he's telling me how much I mean to him. He's *showing* me how he feels about me, in a way *I* can *feel*. There's emotion behind every move, every touch, every stroke, caress and kiss.

Love-making is a ride driven by romance, full of power. It's like being lifted up with the thrusting action of NASA's most powerful booster rocket, full of smoke, fire and upward energy. Similarly, it sends you deep into space, until you don't know where you are; but the thrill is so overwhelming, you don't even care. All you know is that, wherever it sends you, you want to <u>stay</u> there.

Love-making is drinking in your lover's body, from head to toe; lingering on every part not just out of the joy of looking at it and feeling its special texture, but also enjoying the effect you're having on your lover as you lovingly manipulate, tongue, suck, kiss and caress that body part, knowing that each and every part you touch gives your lover a different kind of wonderful sensation.

Anyway, it's a spiritual trip for Craig and me, Love-making. And we take our time, because neither of us wants it to end.

I can't think of anything more loving than what Craig did to me the other night; it was something no one had ever done to me before.

I mean, there's nothing more loving than a man going down on his woman; but when Craig does it, it's extra-special. Its...the difference between cheap wine and a $300 bottle of Chateau Margaux; it's the difference between getting a kiss on the cheek from your brother and a kiss pictured in the most romantic movie scene ever.

But I'm getting ahead of myself...Here's what happened:

We both decided to take a "nap" after work one day, each of us knowing full well that we couldn't wait to get our hands on each other. The true nap, it was understood without saying so, would come when we dissolved into the stratosphere of an orgasmic haze, high above the Earth.

As soon as we'd gotten upstairs, Craig opened the door to the balcony off the master bedroom, letting in the delicious scents of all of the wonderful flowers that were then erupting in a collective Springtime bloom outdoors.

I couldn't undress fast enough, and, in a split second, I was under the covers, *tout nu*, eagerly awaiting the start of our Love-making.

The sun was still out, and so I could fully enjoy watching Craig getting barefoot, then stripping off his shirt (seeing his bare chest, taut stomach and hard nipples really gets me going!), dropping trou, and pulling down his bikini briefs...oh man! (Craig's cock hangs down about four inches when its flaccid, and I just want to take it in my mouth whenever I see it swinging loose!)

I know some women say they aren't aroused by visual stimuli, but my eyes are all over Craig when he gets naked (for the shower, for bed, etc.), and I inevitably get wet taking in the gorgeous view!

(I especially love it when he gets down on the carpet, on all fours, to pet our doggy, Mr. Sundance. I go WILD seeing Craig like that, from the rear, his delectable butt up in the air, his balls and cock hanging down in such a *tantalizing* way. But, I digress...)

Anyway, Craig then jumped into bed wearing nothing but a big, sexy smile and the gold bracelet I'd given him. And, when our overheated naked bodies first touched, waves of goosebumps traversed my body as the scent of Craig's body wafted over me.

With Craig lying on his back next to me, I gave him a quick, hot, wet kiss, like a promise of things to come, while I reached over with my left hand to softly play with his balls, letting my fingers explore every inch of his bag.

Eager to see every inch of him, I pulled back the covers, to watch him reach his full erection. (I *love* making his penis spring to life!). There's no greater tribute to a woman than the reaction you get when you make your man a man!

I gave Craig a smile as if to say *nice boner I gave you, huh?*

Knowing how hot he gets when I play with his balls, I just kept teasing him down there until his hips began to gyrate, his breathing grew heavy and he started to moan.

Debating where I wanted to take things, I only occasionally moved my hand up his shaft to play with the head of his outstanding penis. (Craig is of average height, but there's nothing average about his cock; it's thicker and longer than any I've ever had the pleasure to know!)

With my other hand, I began to run two fingers up and down the crack of his bottom -- something I'd never done to him before, but it really turned him on. He seemed at once surprised and excited by what I was doing to him.

I smiled, enjoying the slow burn I was putting him through.

Reaching over to the nightstand for some massage oil, I began massaging his hard-on, slowly moving my hand up and down his rod, firmly squeezing his cock until it was fully erect, glowing hot, and red as can be. From its head, drops of clear pre-cum began to dribble out, something that always gets my juices flowing, sympathetically!

But, before I could jerk him off (as I had decided to do), he pushed me onto my back and, in a jiffy, he had my legs up in the air, his head buried between my thighs.

"I'm going to fuck you and suck you, all night long," he said, his voice drenched in testosterone. (I love it when Craig talks to me like that!) His words made me weak in the knees.

"Oh," I said, the air coming out from my lips as if let out of a hot balloon, as the import of his words sent tingles coursing through my body. I felt a tickling sensation at the base of my neck, as if he'd squeezed an organ there, causing it to release an intoxicating elixir.

His powerful hands then spread my pussy lips wide open, while he simultaneously held my legs over his broad shoulders with his muscular arms, his mouth encompassing my steaming hot slit, his tongue quickly finding its way around my hard clit, which was standing clear out of its hood.

Craig's surprise attack had awakened all my senses. And, when he furtively slipped two fingers into my vagina, I knew he was close to making me come.

An orgasm quickly overwhelmed me. I realized that our neighbors probably could hear me crying out loud with the onset of my climax, with the balcony door open, but, I was so dizzy with emotion, I didn't seem to care! It was very unlike me.

The next thing I knew, Craig was easing himself into me. His well-developed chest was pressing against my breasts, the warmth of his body encircling me, as he slowly, slowly, slowly introduced his stiff cock further and further into my recesses, finally pressing well up into me, its head extending into the inner regions beyond my love canal.

I couldn't help but close my eyes in delirium as the delicious intrusion sent me into a state of rapture. Out of control now, I forcefully pulled his bottom toward me, to fill myself up with him to the fullest. I was so hungry for Craig's cock!

Lowering his head to my breasts, Craig (without moving inside me yet) took one of my tits in his mouth and proceeded to *titillate* it in *every* way -- laving it wildly, nipping it gently with his teeth, and, taking much of the end of it in his mouth, sucking and tonguing it real hard until I felt the throes of an orgasm building in my middle.

Sensing my condition, Craig began to rock me

slowly, moving his hips expertly, until my climax burst upon me like a tidal wave of pleasure, in a rush of hot cream.

"Mmmm...That's what titties are for!" Craig said in soothing tones. In a flash, however, his mouth was all over my pussy again, his arms forcing my feet over my head.

"I'm going to suck you and fuck you all night long," he reminded, the promise making my body spasm with anticipation.

The passion of his cunnilingual attack was amazing. His tongue was everywhere, his mouth sucking everything. Finally, his long, hot tongue found its way deep into my cunt, laving me so earnestly that I lost it again, screaming at the top of my lungs. (My neighbors must have realized by now what a great lover Craig was, by the symphony of feminine sounds coming from our bedroom!)

Before I knew it, Craig was back in the saddle again, his huge, hot, hard-as-iron manhood now slipping madly from one extreme of my pussy to the other, in and out, in and out, the fury of it blowing my mind.

"Can you feel how I feel about you?" Craig whispered breathily even as his magnificent insertions were driving me senseless.

"Yes, yes," I answered with some difficulty, feeling every muscle in my body begin to tense up (especially in my neck) as Craig tore into me.

"I've never felt you hotter," he continued. "You're like a *three-alarm fire* inside!"

His words were like a spark set upon rocket fuel, sending me right over the edge again, my mind in a state of sweet shock as I was wracked with the unbelievable, *all-consuming* spasms of another orgasm.

That was it. I was gone, a mass of jello, quivering and shaking, and totally at his mercy as he once again threw my legs up in the air and his face dove into my gaping wide, sopping wet pussy, salty and sticky with my cum.

"I don't think I can take anymore," I said, my voice half-pleading for him to stop, and half indicating my helplessness in my desire for him to continue.

This time, he went straight for my clit, furiously tongue-fucking it with such intensity it took just seconds before I felt my body giving in to the ravages of another orgasm, the onset of which was reminiscent of the weightless thrill you feel when a roller-coaster you're riding in drops off its highest peak toward its steepest descent, causing you to scream involuntarily at the top of your lungs as the G forces push your organs to the back of your body.

Craig, in keeping with his promise to suck and fuck me into oblivion, then got on top of me again, his arms slipping behind my back, holding me in a bear hug as he plunged his hard-on over and over into me, the fury of his assault absolutely rocking my world!

"Please, please," I said, gasping for air between words...I was so out of breath by now. "I can't take anymore."

We'd been using the rhythm method, and, unfortunately, this was not a day on which I could enjoy the feeling of Craig's cock throbbing and shooting his jism inside me when he came.

"Come for me, baby," I pleaded, "but *not* inside me."

Craig's deep thrusting quickly sent me over the top one more time before his hip gyrations grew faster and faster and he pulled out, rubbing his swollen prick on my stomach until I felt the heat of his cum shooting onto my belly.

Although he'd come, to my surprise, he kept furiously rubbing his shaft over my now-slippery tummy as if half-crazed with emotion. Rubbing and rubbing, he finally came *again*, in a torrent of cum!

"I can't believe it!" I said incredulously. "You came twice!"

Breathing very heavily now, Craig's arms gave way, his chest resting on mine, his heart beating like a bass drum.

I eased one of my hands down to my belly, and I was astonished to find an *ocean* of man-fluid there.

"Honey, you *covered* me with cum!" I told him. "You're *amazing!*"

Before we both knew it, we were knocked out by the love-making, as if we'd been drugged.

An hour later, our consciousness drifting slowly back up to the surface, our naked bodies still pressed together, I found myself luxuriating in postcoital feelings of love and of closeness.

"Can we just stay like this forever?" I asked Craig.

"Yeah, that would be nice," he whispered.

And in some ways, that experience never did come to an end. Its memory often reverberates in me like echoes in a canyon, bringing with it a flood of warmth and of *love*.

N.V.'s Story: The Body Stocking

My boyfriend is very thoughtful. The other day, for instance, he took me to a lingerie store on a whim. There, he told me to "pick out something nice, or *naughty*, if you prefer." I chose something naughty; a sheer body stocking, with an open crotch. Made entirely of sexy black lace, it covered my body from my shoulders to my feet (pressing my breasts down in a very erotic way). But ⁓ its sexiest feature was an opening in the middle that left my upper thighs and pussy bare, for easy access.

From the time I bought it, I couldn't wait for an occasion to put it on! And then, it arrived.

One day, Tom, my boyfriend, phoned me at the women's clothing store I own, telling me that , after work, he wanted to take me to a movie and then to dinner at a fancy, softly-lit, romantic restaurant. An idea instantly flashed in my head. *I would wear my body stocking under my dress that night, to make things interesting.*

I wasn't sure what effect the body stocking would have on Tom, but I was hoping it would spice things up somehow and get his juices going. I was thinking that he'd have a hard time keeping his hands off of me once he was aware of what I had on (or *didn't* have on).

When he arrived to pick me up at my home that night, he was a bit early and I was still struggling to get into my body stocking. (It took me a few minutes to figure out how to squeeze into it!) Not wanting to spoil the surprise right then and there, I pulled the stocking off my feet, threw my bathrobe on, and quickly rushed downstairs to let Tom in. Raising my eyebrows suggestively and speaking to him in my sexiest voice, I told him: "Make yourself comfortable. I'll be down in five minutes."

I came down the stairs ten or more minutes later, resplendent in a long, sexy low-cut black velvet dress. Upon seeing me, Tom raised his eyebrows and smiled.

"Nice dress," he said in a breathy voice. The dress had clearly warmed him up.

"You see what I'm wearing under it?" I asked in a girlish voice, pulling up the dress to my tummy to reveal not just the body stocking but also the fact that I had absolutely no panties on! My bottom, my pussy, and the tops of my thighs were bare. (By the way, girls -- the whole point of wearing a body stocking is to drive your man wild with desire, so it's no good if he doesn't realize you have one on! That's why I showed it to him, the from start of our evening together.)

"Oh man!" he said, reaching out to pull me toward him by the ass. I playfully pushed him away, however, letting my dress fall back down. Flashing him a smile full of promise, I scurried out the door before he could catch me.

I loved the feeling of being in control; of teasing him with a flash of bare skin, and then making him wait to get his hands on me. I was leading him by the nose; from that point on, I was sure that all he would be able to think of was what he'd like to do to me.

Since we arrived at the movie theatre in just the nick of time (because I was so late in getting ready), there weren't that many empty seats available. Tom suggested we take two that were available in the second-to-last row, up against the far left wall, off by themselves. This was a place where we could have a maximum amount of privacy, so my curiosity was aroused -- although I have to add that it was a Saturday night and the theatre was pretty crowded, so I thought that meant we'd have to be on our best behavior.

As we settled into our chairs, a foursome sat in the seats right behind us. *Shit!* I thought. We can't be naughty now. They'd be able to see everything we were doing.

OK, so the interminable movie coming attractions began seconds after we'd sat down, and then, finally, the movie began. (We'd gone to see *Chicago*, which, as it turned out, was a great mood-setter, with all the sexy dancing in it and half-naked women).

Now, all the while, Tom (dressed beautifully, in a luxurious black and grey sweater -- with nothing on under it -- and soft, plush grey pants with dress black shoes) was acting very much the gentleman. Sitting raptly watching the picture, his head resting in his right hand, he appeared as though he was really immersed in it. His legs crossed, with one ankle resting on a knee, he only moved occasionally, when he wanted to cross his legs the other way.

His left hand was on my right knee, but it didn't budge an inch, or move in any way, so I lost myself in the movie, enjoying the feeling of togetherness we were sharing. We'd pushed the armrest that divided us into the upright position so we could snuggle up against each other.

Then, about 15 or 20 minutes into the movie, at the start of a hot dance number when the audience's attention was glued to the screen and the theatre was fairly dark, I felt Tom's left hand slowly pushing my dress over my knees and up my thighs until my legs were almost fully exposed (although not bare; they were mostly covered by the lacy panty hose portion of my body stocking). His hand was resting high up my thigh, not more than an inch from my bare pussy! The proximity of his hand to my privates made my breath grow faster. My pussy quivered in anticipation of him touching it. Soon, I felt sexy changes happening to me. My pussy lips were swelling, my clit was getting hard, and moisture was growing between my legs as I actively imagined what he was planning to do to me!

Stealthily moving his fingers now so they were deeper between my thighs, I could feel the heat from his large hand wafting upon my pussy (the heat affecting my pussy as if he'd actually touched it, making my labia swell even more). Softly massaging the sensitive tender skin of my inner thigh now, so close to my pussy that he was brushing against my bush, Tom then began moving his fingers in gentle circular caresses, over and over, which made me get *really* wet!

I was thinking how ironic the situation had become. Before, I had thought that I was in control of the situation, having put on the sexy body stocking to make Tom suffer. But now, Tom had turned the tables on me. Now, I was the one at *his* mercy.

Still, I had no clue that he would do any more than just tease me in that way. (There had been

numerous occasions on which he done just that --
sweetly torturing me by getting me maddeningly
aroused, without any hope of satisfaction!)

Adjusting his body now (crossing his legs in the
opposite way he'd had them, his head still in his
hand, his right index finger placed across his cheek
like a serious college student taking in a lecture),
he suddenly slipped his whole hand in between
my legs, the side of his palm pressed right between my pussy lips! My eyes closed involuntarily
and I accidentally let a telltale moan escape.

"Oh!" I said, before realizing I'd better keep
quiet or we'd be busted. Luckily, the music from
the movie was pretty loud at that moment and I
don't think anyone heard me. Tom, in fact,
seemed to be intentionally timing the onset of his
sexual explorations to coincide with a noisy scene,
to mask any sounds I might make!

The excitement of knowing that he might be
planning to make me come amidst all those people
was almost impossible to bear. I was hotter than
I've *ever* been.

I realized then and there that there's something
to being done in public places -- everything feels
ten times more exciting! Knowing I had to stay
quiet as he excited every nerve in my body drove

me absolutely crazy!

Adjusting my dress so that Tom's handiwork was concealed from any prying eyes behind us, I spread my legs wider so he could get better access to my now-aching pussy. (And also so he'd know I wanted him to *finish* what he'd started, and not make me suffer too much longer. I couldn't take much more!)

Pushing my pussy lips apart with the two fingers surrounding his middle finger, Tom then used his middle finger to find my clit (he's a pianist, and so he has reallllly talented fingers). He then began rubbing it slowly but insistently. He knows my body way too well (Tom's a great lover), and he quickly had me wriggling in my chair, in spite of my efforts to steady my body. (I'm not sure but I think the guy immediately behind Tom was watching everything! But I was too turned on to be embarrassed, to tell you the truth.)

At that point, I desperately needed to come. His hand was rea!ly working me over!

Sensing that he had me in a frenzy, Tom started making quicker circles around my clit until I felt an almost *excruciating* orgasm gripping my body. My awareness of the setting and need to be quiet led to a much bigger climax than I'd ever felt before.

My head thrown back, my body vibrating from head to toe, Tom refused to let up on my cunt. I had to forcefully grab his hand and remove it from my slit, because any more from him and I would have screamed out loud!

Quickly pulling my dress back down over my knees, I held it protectively over my legs to keep Tom's hands away from my middle, to gain some time to settle down. I had to close my eyes as the intoxicating pleasure continued to make my *brain* tingle.

A few moments later, once Tom had sensed that I had recovered somewhat, he leaned over and gave me a *really* sexy kiss. It wasn't so much a kiss as it was a statement of: *Ha! I really got you!*

In it, there was also the suggestion that there might be more to come. I say this, because he was somehow *communicating* to me as he ran his hot tongue around and around the full circumference of my lips, sometimes flicking the top center as if it was my clit, the masculine energy and passion of it saying to me: *I love making you come and I might just do it again!*

The movie's first dance scene now over, Tom again played the "good boy," resting his hand on my dress over my right knee, pretending to be engrossed in the onscreen action. That is, until the next musical number began, when he once again focused his attentions on me. (That confirmed my notion that he was actively choosing the loudest, darkest scenes in which to launch his furtive sexcapades.)

His nimble fingers slowly pulled my dress up my calves until it was above my knees. Then, he ran his fingers over the portion of my thigh that was covered by the body stocking, sending shivers through my body and making my pussy crave more attention.

Shifting himself in his chair again to get a better angle (he did it cleverly, so that it would appear that he was simply adjusting himself to get more comfortable), he then pulled the middle of my dress *above* my bush and buried his hand between my bare thighs.

(I got the feeling, by the way, that Tom was getting excited by the sight of the luscious tits, butts and thighs of the gorgeous dancers in the movie making him that much more anxious to do me when the scenes got really suggestive.)

Without wasting a second, he tickled my vulva -- down its entire length and then up again -- ever so softly with his little finger, repeating that over and over again until I almost felt like jumping out of my skin. Unable to stay quiet, I found myself arching my back and neck, my head falling back as I uncontrollably groaned "ohhhhh!"

Out of the corner of my eye, I caught one of the men behind me staring me down as if to say *how dare you!* But, I confidently shot him a look as if to say: *don't you wish you were the one doing this?!*

Dipping his middle finger into my recesses for some natural lubrication, he then took his now-slippery digit and, placing it just below my clit, he expertly made delightful flicking motions over my most sensitive areas, imitating what his tongue often does when he goes down on me. Flick, flick, flick. *Flick, flick, flick,* he continued, in a steady rhythm, until, as he felt me tense up, he increased the speed and pressure until I was on the edge of my seat, gasping for air, coming like mad, writhing uncontrollably, the spasms that much stronger because of my inability to shout (which somehow intensified the feeling).

Knowing that he was driving me crazy, he kept finger fucking me until I had to pull his hand away with all my strength or I thought I was going to die! I could barely breathe!

Again, he acted the role of the innocent gentleman for awhile, until the next sexy musical number arrived. This time, he nestled the side of his left hand into the rift of my pussy and began a sweet fluttering motion above my upper vulva -- his pinky feeling like the soft wings of a butterfly over my marble-hard swollen clit.

I was sopping wet, and, in no time, his incessantly fluttering hand brought me to my third climax. I forget much of what happened next (because my mind was gone after that), but I do remember his talented hands making me come at least *two* more times after that, the last time just before the end of the movie. My seat was thoroughly *soaked* by the time I got up to leave!

Tom told me later that some of the moviegoers were giving us looks as they left the theatre. He thinks they missed much of the flick because they were watching him play with my pussy. But I really think it was too dark for anyone to see very much (other than my upper body contorting uncontrollably). And, anyway, Tom most often arranged my dress so the folds kept my privates and his hand hidden from view.

The movie now over, I honestly had difficulty getting up from my seat. My legs were so wobbly, they felt like they were made of jelly! I could barely walk to the car after what he'd done to me! But, then again, I was certainly a happy camper.

I had wanted to turn the tables on Tom and give him a hand job, or even a blow job at the restaurant, but they gave us a tiny, tight booth that only sat one person per side. (If we had been seated at one of their standard-sized tables, I would definitely have sat beside him and made him come in his pants, or gotten under the table and pulled him out for the best oral sex he'd ever had!)

Oh well...that was not to be. Anyway, he took me to his home after a lovely meal, and Tom, not having had his sexual tension relieved at the movie theatre, immediately ordered me to take off all my clothes...EXCEPT for the body stocking. (I was delighted to see that my body stocking was continuing to be such a turn-on for Tom!)

A bit of background -- I am multiorgasmic, and, so when Tom came alive sexually again, I was like...*yeah!* By this time in our relationship, Tom was well aware that I craved sex much of the time, and that I'd never turn down any of his advances. Actually, until Tom came along, I hadn't met a man who could keep up with me. But, God Bless him, he is just as insatiable as I am.

Anyway, as I peeled off my dress, I was loving

the fact that Tom was taking charge and telling me what to do. I was surprised at how much fun it was to play the part of the submissive sex partner. (I should hasten to add that Tom is always very loving to me, and there has never been anything negative about our role playing. Plus, he's often allowed me to play the opposite role, that of a *dominatrix,* so ours has always been a healthy relationship of give-and-take.)

Dutifully obeying him by stripping down to my bare-bottom body stocking, Tom instructed me to sit on the couch.

"I'm not done with you yet!" he said, his mellifluous voice dripping in sex. "Any time you put on your body stocking, you *know* I'm going to have to *eat* you!" His voice alone made me want to come.

Kneeling on the carpet, Tom spread my legs and threw them over his shoulders. He then stretched my pussy wide open with his hands and gave me the tongue lashing of my life! Oh, man!!!!

"Oh, baby, you're going to make me come," I said, as if pleading for mercy. "Baby!...Baby!..."

Tom's tongue going wild, I couldn't hold out more than a minute or two before I felt a knot of tension build in my pussy, which exploded in an orgasm of *incredible* intensity.

Kissing my pussy lovingly for a minute or two afterward, Tom finally brought his lips up to mine and kissed me (as he always does after making me come), which I thought was very sweet, and not a little sexy. (I could taste my pussy juices on his tongue, and smell my pungent perfume on his moustache!)

Covering me in a blanket, he cuddled with me on the couch while we watched a TV movie, and I felt myself break out into a big smile, thinking: *I've got to tell all my girlfriends to go out and get one of these body stockings!*

I couldn't believe how selfless and giving Tom had been! He hadn't sought his own pleasure the whole night long.

In fact, after we'd gone to bed, he tongued me off one more time before he let me remove my body stocking, to be saved for another night of hot sex. After getting up and putting it in the hamper, I stood, now totally nude, looking at poor Tom, his long, bare, sexy body lying on the bed, sporting the biggest hard-on, with drops of sticky pre-cum dripping from its head. It was time for me to return the favor; plus, my pussy was craving Tom's cock.

Jumping on the bed, I hugged and kissed Tom,

reaching down and directing his nice penis to the entrance of my pussy. He was understandably very hot by then (not having come all night). It was if he was on fire!

Getting on top of him (facing him), I rocked him enthusiastically until he came convulsively. He was yelling at the top of his lungs! (I just *love* making him come inside me!)

I didn't stop bouncing up and down on Tom's cock until he reached out and held me in place, begging me to: *"stop, please stop!"*

I dismounted and lay next to him, both of us breathing heavily. Kissing him on the forehead, I held his body close to mine as we both floated away to La La Land, wonderfully exhausted.

Since that night, let's just say that my decision to buy the body stocking has continued to pay off, in dividends, so to speak. It always brings out the animal in Tom!

If you or your lover don't have one, you don't know what you're missing!

K.T.'s Story: Back To The Cave

Many tens of thousands of years ago, five volcanoes erupted in New Mexico just to the west of what is now Albuquerque, sending billions of tons of lava, thousands of degrees hot, cascading down their slopes.

Huge, black, hole-ridden and impossibly heavy boulders with razor-sharp edges were strewn for miles and miles. They now stand in mute testimony to the enormity of the event that created the high mesa surrounding these dormant behemoths.

Because the rocks are so jagged, it makes climbing to the top of the volcanoes treacherous.

About one mile from these volcanoes (known as
The Five Angry Sisters), the Indians of thousands
of years ago left behind mysterious drawings on
the volcanic rocks that came from these once-fiery
peaks. It seems as if they considered this area
hallowed ground. But, whatever the reason, there
is a spiritual atmosphere that surrounds them,
which you can almost reach out and touch.

Now, one of these awesome giants is especially
near and dear to my heart. It's because of one
specific feature that makes it different from the
rest -- a *cave!*

My boyfriend Rich believes it was used by the
ancient Indians. (The roof seems stained by the
soot of many prehistoric fires.)

I often wonder: if that's true, what did they do
there? Did the cave (to which we now refer as
our cave) have a spiritual meaning to them? Or
did they use it simply for shelter from the harsh
winters and cold desert nights?

To us, the cave has a very *mystical* feel to it.
And, especially nice is the fact that few locals
have discovered it; or, if they have, they don't
seem to have appreciated its breathtaking pan-
oramic view of the city in the valley below and of
the Rocky Mountains some 25 miles away. (We
rarely bump into anyone on our hikes up to the

cave, except the occasional biker, who whips past us innocuously on the erosion-rutted unpaved trails that lead through the many thousands of acres of open land that surround our little slice of Heaven.)

Now...what I'm getting to is a story about the first time Rich brought me up there, early on in our relationship. The memory of that night stills holds a special significance for both of us.

Although I'd been in Albuquerque for many years, I hadn't known about the cave. The first I'd heard of it was when Rich mentioned that he knew of a very special place he wanted to take me to, a place he said I'd have to keep secret if he revealed it to me.

I, of course, was intrigued, and so I readily agreed to the terms. (To be honest, though, I never thought Rich's "special place" would live up to its expectations. I thought Rich was exaggerating its magic.)

Rich and I had gone out several times by then and I was *very* attracted to him, but he hadn't yet made "the move" on me. I won't lie; I was hoping Rich was taking me up there to consummate our relationship. My panties had been wet most of the day thinking about him -- all 73 inches of his muscular body, including his big expressive hands and handsome face -- and so I was more than *ready* for Rich's loving attention! I was praying he wouldn't make me wait any longer!

I dressed for the night in a way that I thought might help speed things along in our relationship. Wearing a light, tight red cardigan (leaving the top two and bottom three buttons carelessly open), a short jeans skirt and sexy macrame sandals (not great for the rugged desert terrain, I confess), I was hoping my clothes would give Rich ideas. My D-cup breasts and my shapely legs are my best assets, and a girl's gotta use what she's got!

Rich wore jeans with hiking boots and a tight-fitting thin black V-neck sweater that really looked great on him (I could clearly see his hard nipples poking up and his pectoral muscles bulging through his top). I could tell, stealing a look at the ample bulge in his jeans, that I wasn't likely to be disappointed in the love-making department; he was clearly *hung!* (The thought made my face burn hot, and a sudden weakness come over me.) The cologne he wore that night also made me high, the moment he gave me a warm hug at my door.

The timing for our first trip to our cave couldn't have been better. It was on a June evening, when the sweet, intoxicating Spring air bathed us in warmth and the scent of wildflowers. Rich said it felt like we were walking through "champagne air."

We held hands as we hiked up the dirt trail that was closed off to all but bikers and hikers. I felt my nipples growing hard and my panties wet as I fantasized about what Rich had planned for that evening. I barely heard what he was saying at times, I was so lost in my loving thoughts. I think I smiled the whole way up the long path to the cave.

What *did* we talk about? I remember Rich talking about the sunset, how colorful it was, with all the brilliant pastel shades blazed across the big New Mexico sky. We talked about how the beautiful day made us feel alive.

And I do recall exactly what Rich said next: "I'm really glad I found you."

I was momentarily stunned; I stopped in my tracks, looked Rich right in the eyes as if to make sure I heard what I heard, and then I rushed over and gave him a big, warm hug, standing up on my toes to better press my face and body against his. I remember thinking I don't want this to end! When we parted again, Rich put his left arm around my waist, and I put my right arm around his, and, suddenly, everything looked more beautiful, smelled more lovely, and felt more fantastic -- the sky, the wildflowers, the breeze...

Rich's two dogs were with us, and their presence was somehow comforting. It lent to a kind of primordial feeling the trip took on. You know -- man and woman returning to the cave, with their trusty beasts protecting them, or something to that effect.

It really felt like we were playing out a role that was deep in our collective unconsciousness -- that we were going back to a place that had called out to us from ages past. Perhaps it was a genetically inherited distant memory that beckoned us there, from the time, generations ago, that we'd spent much of our lives in caves.

The hike up to this particular volcano brought us up to about 7,500 feet above sea level, or maybe a little more, so I was a bit winded as we made the last steep ascent up to the cave's opening. (I was happy that the trail led right into its entrance and we didn't have to climb up the jagged volcanic rocks -- I wasn't dressed for that!)

A strange but nice feeling overcame me as I walked inside. It was almost like entering a protective womb. It was rather cozy, even with its sandy dirt floor. Kicking off my shoes, the cool, soft volcanic earth felt invigorating beneath my feet, and tickly between my toes.

One nice feature of the cave is that it stays warm in the Springtime nights when the New Mexico high desert turns a bit chilly. So, as nighttime approached, the pleasant warmth of the cave was at once surprising and most welcome. It seemed at least ten degrees warmer than the surrounding air. No bigger than a small room, the ceiling height no more than 7 feet at most, I felt surrounded by warmth.

That was a welcome surprise because I wasn't *dressed* for the chill of the high desert nighttime air. I was dressed for *effect*. (In the high desert, nights are often 30 or more degrees cooler than the day.)

I wasn't worried in the near-term, though. Actually, I was thinking the dropping temperature might work in my *favor* -- my goosebumps might provide an excuse for Rich to get real close to me! So, as I turned to face the sunset from the lip of the cave's entrance, I rubbed my arms vigorously, hoping Rich would get the message and take me in his arms.

"Cold?" he asked. (My ruse worked!)

"Mmmm," I purred, continuing to massaging my arms as Rich approached me from behind.

I felt Rich's arms surrounding me, his body heat

and the pleasant aroma of his cologne wafting over me as he touched his cheek to mine.

"Beautiful view," he said in rich, sexy baritone tones. "And the scenery isn't bad, either," he joked, complimenting the way I looked.

I could feel my nipples engorging from the effect of his words, his touch, his scent, the heat from his body, and his wonderful voice. I could also feel dampness growing between my legs, as tingles of anticipation swept through my body.

The view from the cave *was* breathtaking. It's really one of the best vantage points in all of New Mexico, especially at sunset, with all of the hues the western sky (like none other) has to offer. The ethereal and ephemeral light show certainly enhanced the romantic mood of the night. It was as if it was happening just for us. Finally, feeling content in Rich's arms, we watched the sun kiss the Earth good-bye.

"In the mood for some wine?" Rich asked.

"Mmm hmmm," I replied in a voice dripping with female hormones.

Rummaging through his backpack, Rich surprised me by pulling out several chunky candles, which he proceeded to place and light along the cave's mouth, on the rugged and heavy black volcanic boulders that guarded its entrance.

The light wasn't much, but it greatly added to the romance of the moment, as he plunged a corkscrew into the cork of a 1998 Reserve Cabernet Sauvignon...good year...definitely not cheap wine! Pulling out the cork, his chest and arm muscles bulged in way that revealed his masculine beauty and ultimate sexiness; I felt myself grow a bit weak thinking about those muscles being put to use in love-making. I wanted him to take me then and there, but I just smiled, my tongue absentmindedly tracing a line down the middle of my top lip as I savored thoughts of Rich getting intimate with me.

Placing the wine bottle in a divot he made in the sandy soil inside the cave, Rich then withdrew a blanket from his backpack and proceeded to make a comfy spot upon which we both could nestle just within the warm womb of the cave, but close enough to its entrance so that we could fully enjoy the dazzling view of the lights of Albuquerque and all parts north, up to Santa Fe and the purplish mountains of distant Los Alamos.

Sitting down next to Rich, my knees pulled up to my chest, I pushed my body right up against his, making him respond by putting his right arm around me, as he handed me one of two cups of wine he'd poured.

Bringing the cup to my lips, I felt momentarily overcome by its intoxicating, sensuous bouquet. I almost didn't hear Rich's words as he spoke of how wonderful the vintage was. I was lost in the moment, all of my senses aroused. My lips felt swollen and hot.

Sipping a little of that wine, I remember thinking that it felt like the nectar of the gods slipping down my throat. I turned toward Rich and his eyes caught mine. I pulled his head toward me and we kissed as though it was the very first time.

Rich's artistry as a lover was instantly made apparent to me by the tantalizingly light brush strokes of his tongue over my lips, as if his tongue was readying my lips for its entrance, as if it was an act of cunnilingus.

Hearing myself give out a soft moan, I pulled harder on the back of his neck, drawing him closer to me, as if I could not bring him close enough, my other hand reaching down to pull his sweater out from his pants. I wanted desperately to feel his skin, and, especially, his rippling chest muscles.

Rich was driving me wild with his expert hands, both of which had found my nipples through my top; he rolled and squeezed each nipple in a way that made my juices flow down my thighs. It was as if he was milking my nipples and my pussy at the same time.

Losing control, I couldn't move fast enough. Standing up in a mad rush, I had my skirt down by my ankles and my top off in a flash.

Being naked outdoors gave me a feeling of exhilaration. (I'd never done that before!) It felt at once natural and even familiar (as if ancestral memories of cave life were awakened in my brain).

With great enthusiasm, I knelt back down on the blanket. Rich reached out to touch me, but I intercepted his hands. Pausing a split second to tease him, I then took command by pushing Rich down on his back before he had the chance to regain the initiative.

I didn't wait for him to undress; my hands were all over his belt and his zipper; I couldn't get his pants off fast enough. Standing up again, we both laughed as I grabbed the ends of his pants legs and, in a whoosh, tore the pants off Rich.

What made me stand still for a moment was the sight of his enormous hard-on, straining to be released from his blue bikini briefs. Part of the mystery was solved; he was no disappointment!

Back on my knees, I put my hand over his cock and felt him through the thin fabric of his undies, his hardness growing pleasantly with my every touch. Rich began to moan and groan as I rubbed him up and down with one hand as I tickled his balls with the other.

Simultaneously, I felt Rich finessing the hooks on my bra, easily popping them open with one hand. I felt my temperature rising as I anticipated the freeing of my breasts from their restraints. Gently reaching around to pop my breasts out of their cups, he squeezed them together and starting tonguing *both* of my nipples at once.

"Oh!" I gasped, frozen for a second by the electric charge he'd sent through my body. My needs were urgent now.

Pushing him back down onto his back, I whipped off his sweater as if there was no time left to waste, and then ripped off his undies. We both laughed at the urgency with which I attacked him.

But the levity quickly gave way to earnest love-making as I quickly took his cock between my lips, my mouth sliding up and down his thick shaft as my hands massaged his cock and balls. Rich's moans reverberated in the cave as I devoured his God-given gift.

"Oh, I'm soooooo HOT!" Rich said, asking me to: "Please slow down. Let's make it last. I haven't been with a woman in some time, and so my cock is soooo HOT."

Moving back up to his face to hungrily kiss his lips for a few seconds, I then -- thinking *I can't wait any longer --* moved on top of Rich so I could take him into me...*now.* Turning my body so I was facing the exquisite view outside (facing away from Rich), crouching on my feet, I lowered myself onto his rampant erection.

Every inch made me tremble as I eased its huge circumference into my pussy. I was so hot and wet and needy I didn't need or desire any fore-play. The entire length of Rich's hard-on now inside me, I collapsed forward for a second, overwhelmed by the amazing sense of ecstacy that was coursing through my body, now overtaking my mind, swimming around up there awhile before it subsided and I could continue.

My hands at my sides on the sandy soil of the cave, I began slowly sliding up and down Rich's cock. The pleasure was almost excruciating. Before long, my patience ran out and I began bouncing up and down... I needed to *come!* I'd been thinking about this moment *all day long!*

"Ohh," I groaned, as the girth of his cock stretched my insides like they had never been stretched before. The fullness of his cock created sensations I'd never felt before, sensations that built and built until they burst upon me in a rollicking orgasm.

I began screaming as the first waves of pleasure rushed from my hips to my face. I remember being shocked by how rapidly and strongly I'd come. I felt as if *fireworks* were going off in my brain.

Reflecting on the novel feelings the girth of Rich's cock had produced in my cunt, I thought *I guess size does matter*!

Finding it momentarily hard to move much, my vagina over-sensitized by my climax, I just leaned back on my hands, my heart pounding, my lungs breathing deeply and rapidly...it seemed as if the whole *world* was shaking.

For awhile I just rested there, Rich's hard-on still swollen beyond belief in my pussy, his hands titillating every part of my body, with feather light strokes. Reaching up with both of his large hands, Rich then started cuddling and kneading my breasts, which awakened all the nerves in my body. As I started squirming and moaning, his talented fingers began stimulating my nipples, pinching them softly, rolling them, flicking their points... and soon I found myself rocking and rolling again on top of Rich's cock.

My body was on fire. And I couldn't grind my hips *fast* enough. I needed to come again, and I needed to come *NOW.*

Pounding my body down on his swollen member with as much speed and strength as I could muster, it didn't take long before I felt a tickle in my G Spot, which spread to my clit, and then expanded upward until it exploded into a huge head-to-toe orgasm of immense proportions.

Shouting at the top of my lungs, I thought the *world* would hear my climax, as the cave's opening projected my cries out toward the houses lit up in the valley down below.

I became unable to move, my nerves firing bursts of electricity willy nilly, causing spasms throughout my body. Breathing heavily, I then felt something else...a feeling of intense love toward Rich.

Being our first time loving each other, the setting and my emotions just overwhelmed me. I briefly dismounted and threw my body onto his, kissing him over and over and over, everywhere, as if I couldn't kiss him enough.

Easing me up to my feet with our lips locked in a passionate kiss, Rich and I embraced by the cave's entrance for what seemed like hours. Our bodies hot, our arms holding each other tight with the gratitude only lovers can experience, I thought: *it doesn't get any better than this!*

Gently turning me around and bending me over one of the volcanic rocks at the front, so that my hands were resting on its top, Rich then gently placed the swollen head of his cock at my pussy's entrance, in order to take me from behind.

"Oh!" I sighed as he ever-so slowly slid his humongous cock into my sopping-wet cunt. The feeling of being taken from behind was blowing my mind!

I'm not sure if it's true, but as he eased his penis into me, I got the impression that Rich had grown even bigger than he had been before! (I had caught a glimpse of his cock from behind, and it was *extremely* red and swollen.)

"Aahhhhhhhhhhhh," I groaned, surprised that his very first penetration had made me come. (That had never happened to me before; but, I'd never been with such a big man before.)

Next, I felt his powerful thighs press up against the backs of my thighs, his hips tight against mine, as he proceeded to gift me with the most masterful love-making I have ever enjoyed. First making wide circles with his hips (no one had ever moved their cock inside me in that way before), he then teased me by repeatedly pulling his dick out and then slowly reinserting it all the way up to the max. This teasing seemed to go on forever, until I was feverishly hot.

Desperately reaching back and pulling on his hips

rhythmically, Rich instantly understood my need for release, and so he started fucking me with an insistent, steady rhythm -- first at a moderate pace and then slowly building in speed and power, until my hole was wide open, yielding to Rich's furious attack. I came again and again, like I've never come before; Rich had found my G Spot and was playing it like a Stradivarius.

Tens of minutes flew by yet Rich showed no sign of letting up on me. Every thrust of his hips sent me off on a rainbow of incredible sensations. The pulsations in my head were so insistent that I wasn't sure how much more I could take...I'd never experienced such sustained intensity...yet I didn't want him to stop.

Finally, I was so weak that I could no longer stand up; I collapsed on my knees, leaning my head down on my jeans skirt, on the boulder in front of me, Rich kneeling down behind me, not missing a beat.

Suddenly, Rich's wonderful hands were passionately exploring my entire body, arousing my thighs, my calves, my feet, my hips, tummy and breasts. Then, titillating *both* of my nipples at the same time with his large left hand (incredible!), he leaned forward, pressing his warm, hard chest against my back, and started tickling my clit with his right hand. Kissing the back of my neck now, causing electricity to shoot down my spine, Rich's simultaneous stimulation of my tits, my clit, my neck and my cunt made it feel as if TWO or more lovers were making love to me at the same time.

That was it. I could take no more. The full-body assault was too much for me. Plus, Rich's cock was now reaming my pussy with such vigor that I knew he was going to send me off on a *really* huge orgasm.

"Rich...You're going to make me....come!" I managed to blurt out before the onset of a nuclear-sized climax incapacitated me.

"Oh!...Ah!!!...Ohhhhhhhh!" I screamed, Rich's nonstop thrusting making the rush of pleasure rise higher and higher in power until it felt as if I was surfing atop a tidal wave, my whole body shaking, the wind knocked out of me...

I shook for what seemed like forever. Cuddling me from behind, Rich kissed me over and over again as I attempted to come back to Earth. It felt as if he had sent me into orbit, way, way into space somewhere.

My head was still reeling, but Rich's rock hard cock, now pressed up deeply inside me, was driving me crazy. So I began to rock back on Rich, giving it to him with everything I had. I had to make him come.

"Oh!" he groaned, seemingly unable to move. I intensified my attack, wiggling my hips and pounding away like a madwoman until Rich lost it. Our two-hour love-making session ended sweetly with Rich shooting an effusion of hot, wet jism, onto my bare back, like a volcano himself, giving up his pent-up explosiveness.

Afterward, it took me awhile to come back to Earth, so to speak. Still breathless, I looked out over the valley below, and then up to the plethora of stars that now graced the darkening skies, and I thought...man, this is really Heaven.

A noise, undoubtedly an animal somewhere brought us back to reality and we were a bit spooked by it. Rich and I laughed as we desperately looked for our clothes in the darkness, hastily struggling to get our undies on without falling over due to the black of night as well as the dizzying aftereffects of our sexual experience. (Rich actually lost his favorite pair of sunglasses that night; it had been too dark to see them lying there on the cave floor. But -- it was so sweet -- he later told me that it was a small price to pay for such a glorious night of love-making.)

"Doggies!" Rich shouted, realizing belatedly he'd lost track of them, but it was OK; they hadn't gone anywhere. They were dutifully lying at the base of the volcano, looking as if they were taking in the beauty of the scenery.

Walking, hand-in-hand, as best we could (we were like the walking wounded) and as quickly as we could, a near-full moon providing just enough light for us to find our way back to Rich's SUV, I felt bathed in warmth, protected by a haze of love that surrounded me and kept me from feeling the coolness of the night air.

If you're curious, we're still together, years later, still very much in love, our love-making only getting better with each passing month.

But, our experience in that cave is still fresh in my mind, glowing like one of Rich's candles in the cave's darkness. *It was <u>the</u> thing that solidified our love.*

We still journey back along the mildly arduous trek to "our" cave from time to time, to take in the view at sunset. We sometimes consecrate it, too, if you will, through love-making sessions that inevitably bring back wonderful memories of our very first time together.

B.B.'s Story: On The Road Again

Living with Mark has been a revelation. I've done much more with Mark than I've done with any other man, sexually speaking.

I never cared much for going down on a man before I met Mark, for instance. But what I'm really talking about are the WILD things he's gotten me to do, *willingly*.

It just feels natural to be fully sexual with Mark, without the imposition of any restrictions.

OK -- here's another example:

I'd never made love in public places before I met Mark; nor had I masturbated for a man before.

I also had never been so submissive. With Mark, it gets me so hot when he tells me what to do, in a sexual context. Whereas I would never have dreamed of giving in to a man in such a way before, I find myself gladly being totally submissive to him, a slave to his wishes.

Of course, I hasten to add that, although Mark's the most creative lover I've ever had, all of the sexual scenarios he's put me through have been colored with love. It's not hard to submit to your man when you feel the love in his every touch, every penetration, every word.

Actually, what I'm about to tell you began as *my* idea...but it was Mark's supportive attitude and his encouragement of my own experimentation that made it all possible.

It's a little bit embarrassing telling you this, but, the other day, we'd had hot sex in a Santa Fe hotel just before we headed home from a week-end rendezvous, and, as we hit the road, I couldn't stop thinking about what Mark had done to me that morning in bed. I began to get hot all over again as the memories replayed through my mind.

I could feel my pussy growing wetter by the second as Mark directed his SUV down the winding, romantic, tree lined roads toward the highway. There was something about the warmth of the sunshine, the flower-scented air and everything coming alive in the Springtime, and the pleasant, peaceful atmosphere of the towns we were passing through that really got me in the mood for more loving.

I took off my sandals and let out a soft sigh as my thoughts grew more obsessive about Mark. Putting my bare feet on the dash, my black-and-flower-pattern sundress slid carelessly down my thighs until my legs were totally exposed, as I pondered how I might arrange things to satisfy my needs *on the road*.

What would I tell Mark?...To pull over to the side of the road (wasn't that too dangerous, I wondered)?...To take me back to the hotel (too complicated and costly, I thought)?

Mark must have had the same thing on his mind, too, because after he pulled his truck onto the highway (I-25) for the one-hour-long journey home, he began sensually stroking the inner side of my bare knee (with his right hand, unencumbered by the duty of steering). I felt shivers go up my thighs, up to my nipples, my face and the top of my head as Mark expertly caused tingles of electricity to fire through my private nerves -- the nerves that, when touched, make me want sex (those spots whose location only the best of lovers, like Mark, seem to know).

Yet, even as he moved his hand lightly onto my left leg's inner thigh, I wasn't quite sure whether Mark was really going to put out my growing fires, or not. I mean, he was DRIVING on a two-lane 75 mile-per-hour road (going 80)! Could he really do me while he was at the wheel?

The thought that he might continue to make me wetter and hotter without quenching my dire needs only drove me more insane as his fabulous fingers began to elicit soft moans from me. His soft massage work already had my cunt crying out to be touched.

I became more hopeful when Mark pushed my dress above my hips, so my thighs and panties were exposed, my legs wide apart. Unbeknownst to me (my eyes were closed at the time), he then sped up to pass a semi, whose driver must have gotten a good view, because he honked his loud horn suggestively as we passed.

"You did that on purpose!" I said, hitting Mark

on the arm, laughing in spite of my embarrassment (although I made sure not to louse up Mark's momentum -- I made sure to leave my dress as Mark had left it, lying carelessly above my waist).

Mark, let go a guilty laugh, but my resistance to the revealing state he had put me in melted under his persistent assault on my senses. He was now softly making feather-light circles with his fingers, starting on my hips, bypassing my mound, going down one thigh and then across and up the other, causing heat to rise from between my legs up to my cheeks, my nipples hardening as a strong tickling sensation grew in my throat.

A soft "ohhh" passed out of my lips and I heard Mark say "mmmm!" as he watched the effects of his pleasurable tormenting -- the uncontrollable heaving of my body with his every touch. It was almost impossible for me to open my eyes now, but I found the strength to open them just a crack to look at the seam above Mark's zipper, and found, to my satisfaction, that it was bulging out appreciably. (Mark is not the kind of man who can hide his manhood even beneath the thickest pair of jeans!)

I closed my eyes again and gave in to the ardent sensations Mark was causing, his gentle, artful fingers finding their way to my source of agony. At first, he ran his index and middle fingers up and down the outlines of my vulva through my soaked-through panties until they were absolutely slippery wet (later, during a rest stop, I blushed to see, in the ladies' room mirror, that he'd caused me to leave a telltale stain on the back of my dress).

My sweet suffering grew as Mark's ministrations increased in pace, strength and urgency. Closing my eyes again, I pushed my feet against the wind-shield, my head rolling on the head rest, reeling with the effects of what Mark was doing to me.

Then, he startled me, by pulling my panties down my legs and past my bare feet before I was even aware of what he was doing. I opened my eyes in astonishment, but I did nothing but send a half-smile/half-scolding look in Mark's direction. Because being stripped in this fashion gave me the guilty pleasure of feeling an erotic kind of vulner-ability (being half-naked, for all to see, on the highway), and that got me even more aroused.

Somehow, I didn't seem to mind if passersby witnessed my state of affairs. I again leaned back in my seat and closed my eyes, enjoying every moment of it.

Without restraint now, Mark exposed my hot,

wet, inner core to the bathing-warm rays of the sun as he went about driving me absolutely mad. Lubricating his fingers in my cream, he seemed to savor running them, ever-so-slowly, over every outline, cleft and protrusion of mine -- except my clitoris. He knew the effect those explorations were having on me, and he seemed to be getting off on orchestrating my reactions (my hips were now gyrating involuntarily, my body wriggling, my groans becoming louder and louder)...he knew how frustrated he was making me by avoiding the one place I really wanted him to touch now...that is, until he finally, finally, placed his fingers over my clit.

Rolling my achingly-hard love marble between his thumb and middle finger over and over until he made my body writhe uncontrollably, continuing in that way until my shouts became screams. Then he went in for the kill.

Taking two fingers, he rubbed back and forth just like I do when I masturbate, back and forth, back and forth, faster and faster, harder and harder over my clitoris, until this huge tickle grew in my groin, which burst into a orgasm that I thought was going to take my head off. My limbs were thrashing about as I convulsed all over the front seat from its intensity. (From the corner of one eye, I could see that a trucker was keeping up with Mark, in the right lane, watching everything, but, strangely enough, I didn't care! In fact, it seemed to give my sexual predicament an added edge.)

Pulling down my dress, I snuggled up against Mark, my body shaking, my head on Mark's chest, my hands clinging to his shirt, as Mark softly stroked my hair.

"That was nice," he whispered.

"Mmm hmmm!" I responded.

But, a minute or two later I realized I was still in need of sexual attention. I confess to being a bit oversexed; or, perhaps, I'm just multi-orgasmic. Or, perhaps, I just needed his dick.

Whatever. I was still horny! Instead of being satisfied by the day's great lovemaking, it only energized me and made me want more!

I couldn't help myself as my mind raced to come up with an acceptable solution, without somehow offending Mark. (I didn't want him to think, wrongly, that I wasn't really pleased by what he had just done to me.)

Anyway, after I had returned to my seat and casually rearranged my hair in the mirror, I started rummaging through our bags in the backseat, when I suddenly came across what I was looking for -- the sex toys we'd taken with us, which we hadn't had a chance to use that weekend! One of them was my vibrator -- white, the size and shape of a medium-sized erection, with two vibrating speeds and two ways it would wiggle inside of you.

"Oh look," I said, holding up my vibrator (I did my best to pretend as if I'd accidentally discovered it). Feeling a tickle in my throat and an insatiable desire to do myself with one of my toys, I added: "We forgot about the toys we brought!"

To my delight, Mark picked up on my lead and went with it.

"Oh baby," he said in deep, sexy, playful tones. "What should we do to rectify that omission? Maybe you need to do yourself with your vibrator...right now!

"I think your poor cunt is desperate for more attention!" he added, pulling my dress back over my hips as I reclined back in my chair, my vibrator directly over my pussy. (Mark is great about talking dirty to me; some men attempt to get sexy in that way, but it just sounds funny. With Mark, it comes out sounding natural; his words, and the tone of his voice make me want to come!)

With Mark's encouragement, I began working the head of the vibrator up and down my slit. Impatient now to have a phallic-shaped object up and inside of me, I scrunched down in my seat, so that my legs were splayed wide and my pussy was more open and accessible (even though I was more exposed to the view of others). Then, I turned the vibrator on low and dipped the head of the rubber penis into my glistening-wet pussy.

That's when I saw Mark step down on the accelerator harder.

"Let's do a little show for the trucker up ahead," he teased, as pulling up closer to the semi.

"No way!" I said laughing, quickly pulling my skirt down (without pulling the vibrator away from my privates).

Mark smiled devilishly, briefly keeping pace with the truck, but then he sped on past the trucker, and so I felt it was safe to close my eyes and ease my toy deeper and deeper into my slippery hot recesses, doing my best to imagine that it was Mark who was in my cunt. Now pushing the button that turned the motor on high speed, I worked it in and out, in and out, becoming hotter and hotter.

My pussy began to throb and rhythmically grip the vibrator as I quickly arrived at the verge of another orgasm. Pushing the button that turned on the wiggling motion, I started moaning, as the idea of what I was doing, in public, went to my head.

Mark was apparently watching everything, because I felt his large hand cover mine atop the vibrator and then guide it deeper into me so that the clit tickler was right on the sensitive flesh next to my clitoris. That was it. I quickly arrived at a screaming, bucking, frenzy of a climax, my bottom rocking back and forth, fucking the vibrator, to maximize its effect, as I lost all control.

(I'm not sure, but I got the feeling we occasionally passed some vehicles during my orgasm, but, I guess I discovered I'm a bit of an exhibitionist, because I didn't mind that they could see what I was doing. I can't explain it, but there was a sexy helplessness about it: you know, *look at me, I'm so hot I can't help but do myself right now, even if you can see me*. At the moment, my head was spinning and nothing else mattered.)

Somehow finding the strength to turn off my incessant toy, I rested, with the vibrator still up my cunt, for five to ten minutes, half-sleeping, until I noticed that Mark had pulled into a gas station!

That Devil!

There was no relieving myself of my rubber tormentor until Mark was done pumping the gas and we were back on the highway!

On the road again, Mark reached between my legs, through my dress, and tried turning the vibrator back on, but, after we'd wrestled a bit for it, I managed to pull the cum-coated object out from between my thighs, and secreted it quickly into one of my bags, on the back seat.

I can't say I'd recommend that kind of experience for the feint-hearted. But, it strengthened the feelings of love I feel for Mark. (How could it NOT? How many men would be secure enough and sexually liberated enough to take their woman on such a wild ride?!)

When two lovers share something so private, so exciting, so unusual, so *loving* together, it makes for a tighter bond. It's hard to explain what's at work there.

The two of us had just built another little bridge, on a road we hope will last a lifetime.

(And I can't *wait* to get back on the road again with Mark!)

D.D.'s Story: Afternoon Delight

I'd been dating Robert for only a month, but he was such a good lover I was having trouble concentrating on my work. Thoughts about what he'd done to me sexually in the days and nights we'd spent together were playing over and over incessantly in my mind!

I was obsessing about him, actually, and I'd never experienced that level of desire before. I'd reached the stage where I could hardly stand being away from him!

The story I'm about to tell you happened one cold December morning, the day after I'd returned home from a two-day business trip.

I'd already gone to work but, with my mind unable to think of anything but Robert, my panties were already soaked. I realized that it was no use trying to get anything done. So, I decided to call him and take the direct approach. We'd been seeing each other long enough, I figured, to be blunt.

"Hey," I said.

"Hey," he replied.

"I've been wet two days now, and my nipples have been hard since last night," I purred. "I need some attention."

"Oh," he replied, in a breathy baritone voice. I could tell the idea suited him just fine. "When can you come over?" he asked. "Dr. Robert can see you right now if you can get here soon. I've got just the prescription for your problem."

Robert worked out of his home, thank Goodness! I needed him then and there.

Pictures raced through my mind on the long drive over to Robert's house. (Actually, it took only a half hour to get there, but it seemed like the longest half hour of my life.) I kept going through possible scenarios, remembering the many ways in which he'd made love to me before, and the many *locations* (bent over the living room couch, standing in the shower, in the back of his SUV on a high desert mesa top overlooking the city, and in every position imaginable).

When he opened his front door, I could see he was dressed the way I liked him best: barefoot and shirtless, clad only in faded jeans (with the top button undone).

"Come on in," he said, "Dr. Robert is ready."

Smiling broadly, breathless, I practically jumped into Robert's arms, and gave him the biggest kiss of his life.

"Mmm! Mmm!" we both moaned, as we hungrily devoured each others' lips as though we had discovered the juiciest fruit in a desperate journey through a parched desert.

We were *both* in a hungry rush for each other. A second after our lips parted, Robert got this look on his face and, in an instant, he was under my dress, pulling my panties off, and then, as he reemerged, he removed my red pumps.

His arm now around my back, leading me to the washroom, he told me (in his mock serious Dr. Robert voice) to "come this way; we need to hose you down before the therapy session."

Stopping for a moment, I asked him, "wouldn't you like the patient to remove the rest of her clothes?"

"Mmm hmm!" he replied in his fabulous deep voice.

I obediently complied, lifting my dress over my head. Robert reached his arms around me, however, and undid the hooks of my bra, holding my now-nude body in a bear hug as we kissed again. It felt really sexy to be standing there naked, kissing him.

Then, he urgently led me by the hand to the downstairs bathtub, where he took the shower massager off its holder and, turning on the hot and cold faucets, he felt the water gushing from the pipe to insure that it was the right temperature. He then switched on the massager and used its blast of hot water to heat up the porcelain of the tub, in preparation for what he'd planned for me.

It felt a bit naughty, me being totally bare next to him, as he prepared his surprise for me. He had kept his jeans on and it seemed clear to me that he'd not be removing them right away.

"Lie down, and put your feet on the wall, spread apart," he said, pointing to two spots above the faucets where he wanted me to place my feet. I followed his directions, growing excited as I obeyed his every command. Now lying down in the tub, my feet splayed on the wall, with Robert towering above me, I suddenly realized the tub was still a bit cold.

"Cold, cold!" I said in a girlish voice.

"I'll warm you up," he said, still using his Dr. Robert voice.

Turning up the heat of the water, he now directed the spray from the shower massager so that the water was landing in marvelous circular waves all over my body, tickling me everywhere, setting my body on fire. After a minute or two, he began using the spray to stimulate my feet and legs, my belly and breasts, my neck, and then my feet again, in a way that made me feel as if many lovers were loving me, all over my body.

I could hear myself groaning as he then directed the massager's flow into the recesses of my bottom, over my inner thighs, and then, with his left hand deftly opening my pussy lips wide, over the hot soft flesh between my legs.

Overexcited by now (I was, to begin with, hot from two days of fantasizing about him!), I could already feel a climax coming on, and Robert seemed to sense it. Hearing my groans become screams, watching my hands grip the bathtub sides, he *knew* I could stand it no longer.

Now aiming the water so the massaging waves were pulsating over my slit, he started shaking the massager so that the water went rapidly up and down, like he was prepping me to come.

And then...with his thumb and forefinger, he exposed my clit to the direct spray. Turning the faucet handle so as to increase its flow and temperature, the added heat and water power sent me over the edge.

"Ohhh...ahhhhhh...ohhhhhhhhh!" I shouted, shaking from head to toe in the throes of one of the most powerful orgasms I've ever felt. "Oh!... Oh!!..." It seemed to go on forever!

Sitting up now, trying to get a grip, I felt Robert lovingly place a towel over my wet, naked body. Kneeling down to hug me in the tub, he put his head against mine and rocked me gently for awhile, as I suddenly started to cry.

"Why are you crying?" he asked, concerned.

"I don't know," I said, laughing. But I knew. They were tears of release from a really great orgasm, and from realizing that I was in the best relationship of my life.

"Here," he said, getting up to hand me a fresh towel. "Dry yourself off and come upstairs for the next part of your therapy."

As I dried my hair, Robert, still clad in jeans, led

me upstairs to his bedroom. As we entered the room, something told me that Robert had prepared it in advance, that he had something else new and different planned for me!

"Lie facedown on the bed," he intoned.

I had no idea what was coming next, but I obediently laid facedown on the sheets. Then taking a pair of pantyhose I'd left behind from my last visit from under the bed, Robert gently tied my wrists to the bedposts.

As I looked back to see Robert and watched him undoing his zipper, I thought for a moment: *OK, what have I gotten into? Do I trust this guy enough to do this?*

Just then, Robert shot me a warm smile while pulling off his jeans and underpants, and I thought: *I'm going to give in to this. It's probably OK.* Deep down inside, I had always fantasized about something like this happening to me, being out of control and being taken.

Glancing down, I snuck a quick look at him and I was happy to see his cock standing straight up; he was as eager as I was.

Although Robert was 42 at the time, he had the slim, athletic build of a swimmer, with the staying power of a long-distance runner in bed. Just looking at his bare body, 6'1" in height, made me want to come. Plus, he was hung like a horse!

"Get on your knees, so I can put my tongue between your legs," he said softly but insistently. I did so, desperately wanting his mouth on my pussy. The feeling of being helpless, at his beck and call, held in place by my bonds was actually a real rush for me! I could feel my brain excreting endorphins at the thought of my condition.

The touch of Robert's hot tongue between my legs obliterated any other thoughts or doubts. Lying with his back on the bed, lifting my hips with both hands, the tender first strokes of his tongue melted me, making me slump onto the bed. My temperature shot through the roof when his hands split my pussy lips wide apart, pushing my engorged clit up and out from its hood, exposing it to Robert's forays deeper and deeper into my recesses.

"How do you know just what to do?" I groaned, but he didn't answer, nor was any answer required.

Flattening his tongue out, he covered the top portion of my pussy, ever so slowly moving it first to the left, then to the right, and then up and down, teasing me to the point of distraction. I began to wiggle my hips in order to get more pressure.

I did not want to wait much longer; I needed to come again! Getting the hint, he spread apart my lips even wider, stretching them to their maximum (which was a huge turn-on), mercilessly tonguing my clit until I was screaming and coming like I've never done before.

Thoroughly spent, I had to beg Robert to stop. I couldn't push him away, after all, being tied down as I was (which made the experience that much more hot). And, of course, he took advantage of that, didn't he! (Smile.)

"Oh!" I sighed, when he finally, mercifully stopped. I was limp as a rag doll. He laid down by my side and shot me a devilish smile as I attempted to catch my breath.

"Did you like that?" he said, but he didn't wait for my answer; he leaned over and gave me this great, big, tantalizing French kiss, made all the more sexy by the fact I could smell my musky scent on his lips, and taste myself on his tongue.

Pulling away again teasingly, Robert gave me no rest; he clearly had something else in mind for me.

"I've got a new toy for you to play with," he announced, positioning me again facedown on the bed and then anointing the crack of my bare bottom with some kind of oil.

I could hear him opening the wrapper of a

condom, but he didn't put it on himself. He put it around a vibrator (a small, pink penis-shaped one, with a cute little head)! *Omigod,* I thought, *what's he going to do with that?!*

Next, I felt him placing the head of the vibrator against the crack of my bottom, gently going up and down, up and down, without entering me. Then, he turned it on! The thought of being tied down and at his mercy with this machine at his disposal got me really, really wet, and my nipples as hard as rocks.

I'd never had a man's penis or any object for that matter up my bottom, and the idea of that happening made me feel as if my blood was boiling hot. And, then he did it! I couldn't see what he was doing, but I felt him easing the nicely-shaped vibrator slowly, slowly, slowly in, until it was in fully. My head was swimming with a host of pleasures with each inch of penetration, until I thought I was going to come.

I was bucking violently, shouting, groaning, screaming, "Robert! Oh! What are you doing to me?! Oh! Ahhhhhhhh!"

Turning the vibrator up to its maximum now, he cooed to me as he stroked the backs of my thighs and made circling motions over my bottom.

"Do you like that?" he asked.

"Yes," I said, a bit shyly.

But he *knew* I was loving it. He could see me wiggling my hips all over as the persistence of the vibrator drove me wild.

Spreading my thighs with both hands, he then positioned himself so he had access to my pussy. Feeling my labia with his right hand and quickly determining that I was ready for him, he began to ease the head of his huge cock into my crack.

"Ohhhhhhhhhh!" I shouted, from the excitement of being entered from both ends. "You're going to make me come again!"

"How does it feel, being done by two cocks at once?" he asked, but I was too overtaken to respond. "I'm sure you've always fantasized about this," he continued, in sexy, soothing tones.

I had. I had fantasized about that, and it was...it was...grrrrrrrreat!

Wiggling his ass so that his cock moved in circles, assessing my wideness, he finally, in a grand gesture, thrust his cock up to the hilt, firmly holding it there for a second and then quickly pulling it out. The damage was done.

"OH!" I shouted, an expression that Robert instantly recognized as the sound of a woman about to come, because he then madly started thrusting his huge dick in and out of me, twisting his hips a bit with each penetration, until I came and came and came, in peals of sweet agony that echoed off the bedroom walls and out the open windows. I came such in a torrent of hot cum that I could feel it dripping down my thighs (in fact, I could hear my juices sloshing with every stroke from Robert).

My orgasm seemed to go on forever. I was still spasming, thinking he'd remove the vibrator, but he didn't even stop either part of the double-fucking he was giving me! He did slow down, however, now gently moving the vibrator in and out (as if it was being propelled like a second man's cock), his own cock doing my cunt with strong, rhythmic thrusts, until I felt a tickle growing in my bottom, which spread to my cunt, and..."Robert!...Robert! No!!!! Ahhhhhhh!"...he made me come again, *twice*, actually, in quick succession.

But that would do it for Robert. My last orgasm and the vibrations from my toy, which was just a thin membrane from his cock drove him over the edge.

"I'm going to come!" he announced, as his hips pounded wildly, his hard-on reaming the shit out of me.

"Come inside me, baby!" I pleaded (I was on the

pill).

Robert screamed and I shivered as I felt his penis gushing and throbbing over and over inside me.

I'd grown a bit overexcited with the double penetration, and so I breathed a sigh of relief as I felt him pull out of me along with the devilish toy, untying my pantyhose restraints before he laid back as if recovering from a serious blow.

Reaching down to his spent penis, I absentmindedly played with his balls and then jerked a little on his flaccid shaft. Only, to my surprise, his penis unexpectedly sprang back to life!

"Oh, Robert, so fast?" I asked.

Not missing a beat, Robert again rolled me onto my stomach, he placed his legs on either side of mine and insinuated the head of his ever-growing prick into my still-throbbing pussy one more time.

"Oh, no," I said. "I don't know if I can take it!"

"Yes you can," he said, in a tone that was meant to be reassuring and teasing at the same time. Reaching past my hips and around my belly to touch my pussy, he added: "Oh, somebody's wet again!"

And I was. He knew exactly how far to insert his cock before pulling back again, and exactly what rhythm drove me mad. As I grew hotter, he knew precisely how much he should increase the speed of his motion and the depth of his thrusts, until he sent me over the top, three more times.

"OK, OK, OK!" I said, pleading with him to stop. "Stop for a minute!" I needed to catch my breath. "I don't know if I can take any more."

"I never thought I'd hear you say that," he replied in a bedroom voice. He had taken me seriously, and momentarily pulled his hard-on out of my overexcited cunt. But, presently, he began again to tease the outline of my slit, with the head of his cock.

"No, baby, I want to lick you," I said, hoping to gain some down time. Quickly turning around and sitting Robert down on his heels, his boner held tight in my left hand, I whispered: "I need to suck your cock! I enjoy watching you come almost as much as I like coming!"

Quickly repositioning myself, I encircled his engorged shaft with my mouth, opening it real wide to take him all in. (It wasn't easy stretching it that wide!)

Pulling my mouth off of him slowly, as if I was savoring the sweetest lollipop, I urged him on: "Come for me again!" I said, jerking up and down on his shaft with one hand, looking up at him for a moment with a sexy smile, which told him how much I was enjoying now being in control.

Returning my mouth to his upper cock, I began reaming Robert with my lips, with quick down and up strokes, resting a split second at the top to suck the nice head of his cock. His stiffie was like an iron rod, yet the skin of his penis was as soft as velvet. I loved how it felt in my mouth!

I then gave him everything I had, turning my head every which way as I hungrily devoured him. (Any other man would have come by now!) He moaned with every move I made, which was a real kick.

I decided enough was enough; he was going to come, and now! Removing my lips, I vigorously shook his hard-on back and forth, twisting my hand around his shaft, and I could tell I was getting near to making him come.

"Oh, baby!" he cried out, every muscle in his body visibly tensing up.

"Not so fast, buster," I teased. "I want you to come inside me!"

Grabbing his cock and rolling onto my back, I pulled him on top of me, directing his massive boner into my entrance. Robert immediately began working hard to achieve his second orgasm. Over and over, faster and faster, deeper and deeper he went, but he never seemed to stop.

As he went crazy in my cunt, he reached down

and, placing his thumb and index finger on either side of my clit, he started shaking the flesh above my vulva. (It was terribly exciting, because no one had ever done that to me before! And it caused such powerful tingles to grow in my clit!)

With his other hand pinching my nipples (just like I like it), it didn't take long before the combined effect of everything Robert was doing to me sent me off on a thunderous orgasm.

"Robert!...Oh!...Ahhhhhh!" I shouted, my screams practically peeling the paint off the walls. All the while, Robert kept fucking me with just the right rhythm and force to make my pussy tense up, making another orgasm explode inside of me.

"Robert!" I gasped, feeling like I could take no more. "Please...please...come for me!" I said, not wanting to admit he'd pushed me to my limit. "Come inside me, honey! Come for me!"

And my words seemed to have their desired effect...

"OK, baby, I'll come for you...only for you!" he replied, in heated tones.

And then it happened. In a matter of seconds, he was cursing and screaming and bucking and shooting off inside me...It was *fabulous!*

Collapsing in a heap next to me, he joked: "Not bad for a *quickie!*"

Quickie? We'd be going at it for almost two hours!

My body shook for well more than half an hour after we'd fallen quiet in each other's arms, laying side by side, facing each other.

Gazing up and down at his beautiful, bare body, lightly caressing his hips and then playing with his still-hard nipples, I was thinking how lucky I was. It compelled me to confess: "Until you, I never thought I'd find a man strong enough to satisfy me." It was hard not to fall in love with a man who was so loving, and so good to me.

At that moment, I knew I was in trouble. I realized I'd finally met my match.

"I promise to follow you to the ends of the Earth," I gushed. (Only a woman who's ever had her brains fucked out, who's found her dream lover, would understand my emotions at the time.) "And I'll never ever give you a hard time, I promise. Not often, anyway!"

We both laughed.

Ever the romantic, Robert, wearing just a thin silk robe, then made me stay as he whipped up a gourmet lunch of hummus and Greek chicken with spinach. (He's a *great* cook!)

Sitting right next to him as I enjoyed the meal, my face glowing hot, my head dizzy, I had some fun with Robert. I pulled his robe open and ran my fingers along his thighs, until I finally got a rise out of him.

Tenderly wrapping my fingers around his reinvigorated cock, I leaned over and gave Robert a big wet kiss, lightly flicking the front of the head of his cock with my thumb.

"Umm...umm," he moaned.

"I gotta go!" I said, suddenly pulling away from his lips in a big tease. "Stay just like that," I added, nodding my head toward his swollen member, as I ran toward the front door. "I'll be back as soon as I can!"

Giving me a mock scolding look, Robert ran after me. I laughed as I gave him a quick kiss at the door; his hard-on was making his robe stick out like a tent! Poor guy!

Opening the door for me, Robert sent me on my way with a big smile, nearly three *hours* after I'd arrived.

Back at work, my employees commented wryly how happy I seemed that afternoon. And they kept asking me why I was smiling so much (although they obviously *knew* why). Why *indeed!*

N.N.'s Story: On The Wild Side

The trust factor is one thing that makes sex in the early stages of a relationship feel a little...well, *dangerous*, and because of that, it always has a unique *excitement* for me...

Especially if your lover takes you to the edge of your comfort zone. ...Like the first time I went out with Peter (a private investigator whom I'd met through my girlfriend Mary, who'd been a childhood friend of Peter's)...

Peter had taken me to a romantic

night spot for dancing to sexy salsa music. The music was hot and our suggestive, rhythmic body motions, dancing together so closely, had worked me up into such a state that I was thinking thoughts I knew I should not have on a first date.

I blame it partly on the music, which reeks of promised intimacy. I was also under the influence of a few glasses of luscious red Rioja (Spanish) wine, and after a couple of hours of brushing up against Peter on the dance floor (especially, feeling his hard-on through his pants when I pressed my hips against his middle during slow songs), I was burning up inside.

I blame my heightened sense of desire also partly on what I had on (or *didn't* have on!). I had worn a short, eye-catching backless black dress, without a bra. The fabulous fabric was so silky soft that it was constantly stimulating my bare nipples as it brushed up against me, as if the dress were a lover. Its nonstop stimulation kept my tits hard as Peter and I moved to the music. Plus, the dress was so light and soft, it felt almost as if I was totally naked, which gave me the feeling of being kind of naughty!

I had worn that dress to show off my shapely legs, which always turn men's heads. Going braless was my way of turning up the heat another notch under Peter (of whom I'd seen a picture beforehand; he was *gorgeous*). To cap it off, I wore strappy stilettos that showed off my comely feet (and, toward the end of the evening, I kicked them off and danced barefoot).

As you might have imagined, though, I ended up turning myself on as well as Peter, by what I wore. So, yes, that had something to do with my being so aroused by night's end.

But there was another reason, too. There was something about the look in Peter's eye, his masculine scent, his power, the bulge and hardness of the muscles in his arms and chest, and his prowess as a dancer that made me feel I needed to have him inside me. Watching his suave moves on and off the dance floor, I *knew* he'd be a great lover.

Plus, everything about him said *class*. His red silk shirt, his fine black shoes, his velvety-soft black trousers, all spelled money. But it's not the money aspect that got me so hot; it was the feeling that this man was accustomed to the finer things in life, and that everything he did reeked of sophistication. I was helplessly attracted to him.

We must have danced most of the night away, lost in each other's eyes, but we eventually took a break and talk inevitably drifted to sex (which was, I admit, the only thought on my mind at the time). With the driving, sensual rhythms and the romantic lyrics (which Peter translated for me, whispering in my ear as we danced), it was hard for my thoughts not to dwell on that topic.

I surprised even myself when I heard myself unabashedly confessing to Peter what my most intimate fantasies were...Knowing full well the effect it might have on Peter, I told him I was bored with the lovers I'd been with in recent years... that I wanted a man to take control, even tie me down occasionally, spank me from time to time, and make me feel like he was "taking" me.

"Oh, so that's what you want?" Peter said, his eyes sparkling with mischief. "Well then, I think you came to the right man. I have something in mind for you later on, if you don't think I'm being too forward."

Normally, I'd never even consider having sex on a first date, but I was so far gone by this point, I was so taken by Peter, that I couldn't help myself. I wanted him...and *now!*

"Let's not wait! Let's do it now!" I said with a smile, the boldness of my words surprising even me.

Looking at me for a moment, to see if I was being serious, Peter then gave me a flirty smile. Taking me by my hand, he led me to the door, and his car.

Inside his late model sports car, the roar of its engine, the smell of its new leather seats and Peter's proficiency shifting gears with the stick got me hot all over again as he drove me home. I felt like taking his fingers and placing them on my sopping wet crotch to show him what he was doing to me, to let him explore my inner recesses so he could make me melt away in rapturous pleasure.

When Peter pulled into my driveway and leaned over to kiss me, I wholeheartedly kissed him right back. His lips were so soft and sensual, his tongue so experienced, that my cunt quivered in anticipation, demanding immediate attention.

"Mmm, mmm!" I moaned, my passion raging out of control, my hands exploring every inch of Peter's body -- his chest and his nipples through his shirt, his cock, already hard, through his pants... Which I guess made Peter more bold because I felt his hands boldly lifting my dress up to expose my breasts (in my *driveway*, where neighbors could see us!). Soon, in fact, he had my dress over my head and off, thrown into the back seat, his hands lovingly lifting my legs up, placing my feet onto the dash, deftly pulling my panties off and spreading my legs wide for better access as he squeezed, tickled, pinched, caressed and teased every part of my body, our lips still locked in a pussy-wettening kiss, when, suddenly, he backed away from my face a couple of inches and whispered: "What do you think about what I said before? About doing something *wild!* Do you *trust* me?"

"Do I *trust* you?" I said, smiling, but cocking my head a bit, uncertain where this was going.

"Do you *trust* me?" he repeated.

"Should I?" I responded playfully, but a bit nervous now.

He coyly didn't answer.

"Would you mind if I blindfolded you?" he asked, his eyes hinting of exotic delights.

"You want to blindfold me?"

"Yes," he said, with such a sexy and disarming smile that I found myself smiling right back at him and saying softly, "OK!" (My look also said to him: be *good*, now!) I figured, hey, I'm in my driveway; I'm in a safe zone.

Taking out a colorful bandana from his glove

compartment, he gently blindfolded me and started kissing me all over: first my thighs, and then the sensitive, tender skin just inside my hips, then my tummy (where he inserted his hot tongue into my belly button and made circles around it as if it were my pussy), and then my breasts, my nipples, the exquisitely tingly places on my neck... He was lighting fires all over my body...I was gasping, writhing...and then, all of a sudden, I felt him take both of my wrists in one of his strong hands, while he handcuffed me to the handle above the passenger door with the other!

I shuddered -- it happened so quickly, and here I was, totally at his mercy! But at the same time, it felt really exciting.

"What are you doing Peter?," I asked, panting from everything Peter had done to me.

"Do you trust me?" he whispered into my ear. "I'll release you right now if you feel uncomfortable."

Not wanting to spoil the likely harmless fun, I replied: "No, I trust you, Peter." Part of me was thinking, though...*hmmm...I wonder if this is smart?...*

But the other part of me was actually *enjoying* the feeling of helplessness that came over me...I was so wound up sexually, and Peter was "taking" me just like I'd told him I'd always wanted a man to do.

"I want our first time together to be a memorable one," he said soothingly. "I want you to get wet tomorrow when you think about what I've done to you tonight. I want the memories to get you hot all over again, so you want me badly."

He urgently stroked the length of my body, from my vulnerable neck, down to my feet, as he spoke about what he would do to me that night. His feather-light touches drove me crazy, making me squirm in the seat voluptuously.

"Now, nothing feels more risque than to be bare in public, which is what you are," he continued. "And nothing is more exciting than to mix sex with a feeling of danger and of being pushed beyond your boundaries. So...let's take a ride!"

"But," I protested, "everyone's going to see me!"

"Maybe so," he said softly. "But you might even like it!"

"Peter..."

"Here's what I'm going to do to you," he said, cutting me off, and making me listen (I was in no position to protest, and so it was better to listen at this point, to see what he had in mind. To be honest, though, my pussy was getting wetter as the riskier and naughtier aspects of my position sunk in. My cunt was spasming and I felt I would have come in a second if Peter had simply touched my clit.)

"I'm going to drive you to a place where we can be alone and undisturbed," he said, "a very romantic place, with a view of the entire city and its shimmering lights. And I'm going to make love to you like you've never been made love to before."

He described where we were going, and I instantly knew that we were heading to the mesa above the city, and so I began to relax. It wasn't too far from my home, and I knew the territory like the back of my hand. I'd walked my dogs up there many, many times before. And Peter promised to uncuff me once we got there.

But, as we left the paved road and the washboarding of the dirt path shook the car, Peter threw one more curve my way. Lowering his window, he told me, "I'm throwing your dress out the window now...and now...your *panties!*"

I heard a fluttering of fabric in the wind outside his open window as he let them go into the night.

"Peter!" I said, feeling as if I was swooning. I couldn't believe it, but what he'd done had made me a bit scared, but also really, really *turned on!* I never felt so sexy, so naked before. I got so wet, I was soaking his leather seats with my pussy juices (I could feel a wet spot on the seat). I could feel my wetness flowing like a stream down my thighs.

"How do you feel, Senorita?" he asked, in a testosterone-dripping voice.

"Too hot," I replied.

"Good," he said. "I'm going to park here and make love to you the way you said you liked it."

"Ohhh!" I sighed. It felt as if his words were like hands stimulating all of my sensitive places.

In a matter of seconds, the car lurched to an abrupt halt and I heard the ratcheting sound of Peter's parking brake, and the opening and closing of his door. Then, I felt the cool wind of the mesa inciting every nerve on my bare body as Peter whipped open my door and, grabbing me by the hips, guided me (still handcuffed) to stand up, as best I could, right outside the door, facing his car.

The coolness of the sand beneath my bare feet sent sensual shivers through my body, my nipples engorging so much that it hurt. Gently bending me over, I felt two quick slaps on my behind.

"That's for making me so hard while we were dancing!" Peter said (his hand brushed up against my pussy when he spanked me, which got me even more excited).

"Please!" I said, too hot to go on much longer without relief. "Please make love to me!"

"Are you real hot?" he said teasingly.

"*Too* hot!"

"OK!" he said firmly.

And, with that, I heard him kneel behind me, and then I felt his wet tongue probing the cleft between my legs, his hands stroking the backs of my legs, from my bottom down to my feet.

"Oh Peter! Oh!" I sighed. *"Yesss!"*

"You like that?" he whispered.

"Yes, Peter, *yesss!"*

I then felt his tongue vigorously lapping up and down the length of my slit, licking up my juices as he purred "mmm!" Then, I felt his tongue darting *inside* my pussy. His tongue was so long and expert that he soon had it on my G Spot and was driving me wild.

"Peter...Peter...ohhhhhhhhhhhh...ahhhhhh!" I screamed.

I felt one of his hands go between my legs, and, within a second of his finding my clit, I was coming all over his face. The orgasm really knocked me for a loop, it was so strong. It even made me feel a bit *dizzy!* (I'd never felt that way before.)

I wanted to lie down, but I was still handcuffed to the car. Unable to stand up any longer, I collapsed to my knees, made weak by the after-affect of my climax.

Although I was woozy (still attempting to catch my breath), it was nice to feel Peter kissing my back, my buttocks, and then my legs and bottoms of my feet. Kneeling behind me, Peter, still fully clothed, held me tightly to his body, kissing me fervently, while whispering, "I am so glad I found you; you're an angel." As his hands began caressing my belly, my hips and thighs tenderly, I felt the fires stirring inside me once more.

Pulling me up to a standing position once more, I felt Peter's hands feeling my body all over. And then, he mercifully removed my blindfold.

"There!" he said triumphantly. "You're in quite a predicament, aren't you?...Still trust me?"

"Yes, Peter. I do!"

"Good! I thought you'd enjoy the view from here."

Leaning down again behind me, I felt Peter kissing my bottom, his hands spreading my cheeks. Then, his tongue was going wild over the crack between my cheeks, sometimes inserting itself briefly in its outer inches. The feeling was at once surprising and very erotic.

"What are you *doing* to me, Peter?!" I asked, as lovers do, when their partners are blowing their minds.

"I'm making love to you like no man has before," he answered. I felt a glow overcoming my body as I realized for sure I was safe in Peter's hands.

The illusion of danger had worked its magic; but now, I was so overheated that what I desperately needed was Peter's stiff dick between my legs.

"Peter...make love to me," I pleaded.

"Sweetheart, that's just what I'm going to do."

Removing his shoes, socks, pants and bikini briefs, there he stood, still in his shirt, his huge cock fully erect, removing an *Extra Large* condom from his pants pocket. My eyes wide, I wondered if I could take all of him in. He was sooo humongous!

Swiftly unrolling the sheath over his immense hard-on, he then bent over to remove a key from his pants, using it to undo my restraints. Massaging my wrists to make sure they were OK, Peter then planted a sultry French kiss on my lips while hugging my bare body to his with such passion I thought I'd not be able to breathe.

Then, turning my body back around, he gently bent me over and guided my torso down onto the hood of his car, flattening my breasts against its shiny smooth surface. The warmth of the engine on my bare breasts and tummy and the sensation of being naked outdoors got my juices going again, just as Peter guided his impossibly large cock from behind into my still-dripping cunt.

As he penetrated me inch by inch, careful not to hurt me, easily surmounting the tightness of my twat, I noticed headlights coming down the main path we'd taken earlier.

"Peter! There's a car coming!" I said, concerned we'd be seen.

"Let them have a show," he said, holding my neck firmly in place, not stopping for a moment as he began to ream my cunt like it had never been reamed before. I had secretly always wanted to be "taken" like this; the fantasy had seemed terribly sexy...and, in practice, I was not disappointed. Surrendering to a lover in such a primitive way is so hot!

I think I saw the couple in the passing car looking at us as they passed by, no more than 50 yards away, but I wasn't sure (it was a moonless night and it was pretty dark, but I wouldn't be surprised if they had caught a glimpse of something). But somehow, the idea that we might have been caught in the act, and that we were vulnerable to being seen again by another passerby, only made me want Peter more. Strangely enough, I did not feel ashamed; it felt curiously natural to be making love out in the open.

My eager cunt swallowed up as much of Peter as it could take, and then I felt his cock head go beyond my love canal, tickling my cervix. He then began this thing where he would pull back from my cervix just an inch or so and then insert his cock in again, over and over again, until I felt an unfamiliar nerve balling up in my tummy. The feeling was growing and growing in tension, I finally came in a thunderous climax. (Luckily, no one could hear me screaming!)

Feeling a bit light-headed, I really felt like sitting back down in the luxury and warmth of Peter's car, but Peter was really worked up and he started violently pounding my pussy, loosening me up again and, to my surprise, sending me over the top two more times before he exploded inside me in his own cataclysmic climax.

Turning me around and kissing me over and over, we held each other close until the languor-

ous postorgasmic feelings made us rush to the car,
for much-needed rest. Watching the city lights
with Peter, my naked body curled up against him,
in postcoital repose, was one of the most fantastic
things I have ever done in my life.

Later, on the way home, I continued to cuddle
up against Peter, not even worried about the fact
that I was still nude, and someone might see me
on the roads that led to my house (it *was* awfully
late, though, and the streets were pretty deserted).

A pleasant warmth had overtaken me. I was
basking in the afterglow that comes with great
love-making. And I was experiencing feelings of
gratitude and affection toward Peter, as you do
toward a lover who really knocks your socks off.

Inside my garage, the door securely down, Peter
surprised me by returning my dress and panties to
me. He hadn't really thrown them out the window! (But the ruse worked in opening me up to a
wilder side of life and love.)

Since then, Peter and I have become quite close,
our ever-surprising love life a big part of what
makes life with Peter so satisfying.

D.W.'s Story: Tantra-lizing Sex

My boyfriend and I are orgasm aficionados. If you're like me, a student of love-making, so to speak, whose goal is to achieve the highest spiritual and sexual peaks possible through great sex, you arrive at some very valuable insights during this process of discovery.

One of them is that there are many different *types* of orgasms -- from soft to earth-shaking, from quick to deliciously long... And I want to experience *every* kind, especially the ones on the upper end of the scale, which so few people will ever achieve. Because, to achieve them, you have to be a great lover, and be coupled up with a great lover. You have to know how to prolong sex to its absolute limits. And you have to have the spiritual and emotional elements involved as well.

The orgasmic experience is very multicolored. How you feel while in the throes of a climax, for instance, depends upon what body part or parts set it off. There are clit orgasms, G Spot orgasms, neck orgasms, titty orgasms, spinal cord orgasms, deep vaginal orgasms. If your lover's really good, he or she can make you come by stimulating any number of areas on your body, and they'll often send you off on orgasms that they trigger from two or more sensitive areas on your body at once.

(For example, a man can come from your stimulating several different areas: the head of his cock; his shaft; his nipples; his prostate; and his bottom. Don tells me he even had an orgasm that started in his *balls* once, when he was experimenting with his shower massager.)

A smart lover will wait until you're about to come before they pull out all the stops. They'll let you get near the verge, and then they'll add something that'll send you over the top, like a finger up your bottom, or a tongue on the back of your neck or spine.

One neat thing I recently discovered was that my lover could come if I just tickled his *prostate*. (I didn't even know where it was *located* in a man's body until recently. It's about one to two inches up his bottom, behind his privates.)

I learned about it almost by accident. I had found his stash of old Penthouses and Playboys in one of his dresser drawers, and I immediately sat down to look at the pictures and then read the letters that had been sent to the editor of Penthouse.

In one of them, the writer said a female nurse snuck into his hospital room, and asked him if he knew that "a girl can make a guy come by sticking her finger up his bottom, if she knows how to do it." Convincing the patient to roll over on his stomach, she then used some K-Y Jelly and, to his surprise, she fucked him in that way until he came. He said it was the biggest orgasm he'd ever had, and since then, he'd craved being fucked by her.

I don't know if that story was truly a letter from a reader, but I later spoke to Don about it and he confessed that he'd indeed had a lover (a female doctor) who'd once made him come simply by fingering his prostate. He also told me that this gave him his most intense and satisfying orgasm ever. My curiosity, to say the least, was piqued.

So I immediately made Don strip for me, get up on the bed, sit on his heels and then lean forward, kind of like a kneeling fetal position (seeing him that way was so *sexy*). I sat behind him on the bed (with a great view of his balls), and put a dab of Vaseline jelly on my middle finger. Then, I slid my finger up his nice butt while jerking him off with my other hand. That REALLY REALLY drove him wild! When he came, he shot TWICE as much as he normally does! And he screamed louder than I'd ever heard him scream before.

Later, I learned that I could get his prostate going during sex by rubbing the base of his bottom. When I do that, he's told me, it kind of balls up inside of him like a tightening muscle, and, when he comes, it feels like his head is exploding.

But, the point is, Don and I are into exploring all *kinds* of orgasms, from all of our many body parts. We're always experimenting.

Just the other day, for instance, Don caught me off guard by taking one of my vibrators and sliding it into my bottom while I was fucking him, on top. That made me feel like my head was coming off when I came! It absolutely DOUBLED the intensity of the experience!

But -- that being said -- even the level of sophistication we had reached was not enough to satisfy us once we had been initiated into the joys of *tantric* sex, which is what Don and I have gotten into lately. That practice has brought us closer as lovers than we'd ever imagined.

We're not experts by any means. But we kind of got into our own version of tantric love-making after one of my girlfriends told me about it and I did some Internet research into it.

The basic idea is you're supposed to extend your love-making for an hour or more, until it's almost excruciating NOT to come. Then, when you come, you orgasm with every atom of your being. You feel like you're going to pass out.

I can honestly say that I never felt such strong climaxes until Don and I got into this. But, more than that, nothing makes you *love* your partner more than when you making sex go on for as long as you can, savoring each and every feeling, each and every touch, each and every nerve impulse, each and every change your body goes through.

So, for us, tantric love-making has been a magical experience. I mean, the first time we tried it was so exciting, we couldn't wait to do it again!

Don set the scenario (he's great at games and role-playing). He's got this 5-CD changer, and thousands of CDs, and he told me he was going to put 5 of his sexiest CDs in there (they turned out to be CDs by Enya, Barry White, Marvin Gaye, Enigma and Prince), and he was not going to stop fucking me or let me come until the last note sounded.

Can you imagine what THAT was like?!!! It was like...nothing else I'd been through. It was easily the most exciting experience I'd ever had in life up to that point. And it was a real challenge to pull off, let me tell you!

He set the stage by making our livingroom a love nest. He moved the glass-top cocktail table to one side and laid down a blanket on top of the rug, surrounding that area with lots and lots of candles; the stereo's speakers were right at our feet.

He then put a porno movie we'd bought into the DVD player, and let it play, to add to the sensual stimuli. (Hearing someone else come is really hot!)

Then, we simultaneously stripped each other and Don took me by the hand and laid me down gently on the blanket, on my back, my legs set wide apart and my knees bent, my feet flat on the floor up right near my bottom.

"Close your eyes," he whispered, and I obeyed, anxiously awaiting what Don had in store for me.

Lying on his stomach, his head hovering above

my already-dripping-wet pussy (I could feel his breath between my thighs), Don began what, to this day, was the longest, slowest, most painfully pleasurable experience I've had getting cunnilingus.

Don warned me as he started: "I'm REALLY going to tease the shit out of your pussy...I'm REALLY going to take my time in sucking and kissing and laving your sweet pussy!"

I can't say I timed it, but I do know that we listened to one whole CD as he explored my cunt from top to bottom, from inside to out, with his hot, long, wide, and talented tongue...and even then he wouldn't let me come!

Starting so lightly I could barely feel his touch, his tongue first softly tapped and then rested on every fold, curve, nook and cranny of my aching cunt. Then, flattening out his tongue, he covered most of the length of my slit, only slightly moving up and down, up and down. I was already burning hot, and my juices really began to come down.

From then on Don kept me on that plateau. He wouldn't let me get too close to a climax, or he'd instantly back off and slow down even further. It was as though he'd set a burner flame just so, watching its effect on me, lowering it before I came to a boil.

"Mmm," he'd say, as he licked up every drop of honey that came down as the result of his efforts. (The sound of him relishing all of that making me that much hotter.)

Sometimes, he'd push my legs up above my head, holding both of my feet together with one hand, as the wonderful fingers of his other hand stretched my labia to their limit (making me feel as if I was going to lose it right then and there), so he could have better access to my G Spot and clit.

All the while he was stimulating my most sensitive parts, he never sped up much. It was just like "flick-flick-flick!" with his tongue (sometimes in time with Barry White's slow, smooth song rhythms), and then he'd move on to a different spot to set it on fire.

At one point he inserted two fingers in my vagina and just rested them on my G Spot, as his lips sucked my labia delightfully. He was clearly a pussy connoisseur -- he was loving every second of it. (And so was I!)

The extreme nature of Don's tongue movements -- his slow, slow, slow insertions into my recesses, and his lllllllong explorations of my most intimate outlines and shapes -- exacerbated their effect on me.

I was eventually so wound up that I had nearly

passed out by the time Don gently, gently, gently introduced his cock into my hot, hot cunt. I almost came with his slightest movements, as he prolonged his initial penetration for what seemed like minutes.

For awhile, he was just content to keep my pussy fully stuffed, his more than ample cock inserted all the way up my cunt, straining to go ever further. I initially wanted to grind my hips against him because I was dying from the heat, but his strong hands held my hips in place, and he commanded me (lovingly) me to: "Lie still! Let's just get off on the feeling of being united."

So I gave up my natural inclination to work toward an orgasm, and in doing so I found that the whole experience felt totally fresh and new and exciting, in a way I'd never felt before. I realized then that traditional sex, in its rush toward a finite goal, overlooked an important part of love-making -- the joy of just being joined together, in this awesome way.

"I'm really getting off on the feeling of being hard inside you," Don whispered over my left ear. "I don't want this to end."

I reached behind Don's muscular back and gave him such a strong hug I was surprised he didn't break! What a loving thing to say!

He, in response, pushed his arms under and around my back, and we both hugged and hugged each other for several minutes. It was as if we were discovering the miracle of sex for the very first time, and *true love.*

(After all, is it the person who guzzles down a glass of wine who's a connoisseur? No! It's the person who delights in siphoning the liquor off slowly, slowly, slowly, luxuriating in its flavor, drop by drop, who truly appreciates it.)

Since we love teasing each other, we both thrilled to the slow pace we'd chosen to take, and the sensations only such a pace can give you. You *really* enjoy your lover's every touch and its effect on you when you're not goal-oriented. When you're not in a rush to come, when the purpose of what you're doing isn't goal-oriented, it maximizes your appreciation for the second-to-second kaleidoscope of feelings your lover is giving you.

For the next hour or so, Don only moved enough to keep his erection nice and hard and my pussy nice and wet. We began to tell each other all of the many things we were loving about the other during this wondrous ride into unchartered territory. It was truly magnificent!

At this point, I no longer felt hungry to come; I desperately wanted our union to go on *forever.* I was really getting off on being so close to Don, the feeling of his body heat caressing my bare skin, how the ripples in his muscles felt on my body and how his big, hot, hard cock made me feel inside.

I've never felt so wonderfully, joyously *naked*. It had never felt so good just to be a woman. I felt the sensation of being complete for the first time (because I really feel a woman and her man are just two halves of a whole). I felt...*love,* rushing over me.

At some point, Don began tantalizing me with almost imperceptible cock motions -- outward slides that seemed to last an eternity; insistent forward insertions that moved at a snail's pace; side-to-side tickling and sllllow circles, all of which raised my level of desire to a feverish pitch.

The sounds coming from the erotic DVD (the squeals and cries of a woman being driven mad by her lover, and then the explosion of screams as his cock pushed her over the edge) started to get me too hot to go much further. After awhile, I heard myself begging Don to finish me off.

"I can't take any more," I said pleadingly, panting deeply, trying to get release by grinding my hips on him.

But, he wouldn't give in so easily, and so he kept me just below the boiling point for another half hour or so until I could tell by the quickening pace of his cocking that he too had taken more than he could bear.

Don's a former athlete, so lasting the length of those five CDs wasn't a problem physically; nonetheless, neither of us could go the distance.

Finally achieving a pace and intensity that pushed us both over the top, we bucked together in the heat of the moment until we both achieved the biggest orgasms of our lives.

When I came, every organ in my body was throbbing, my head was reeling, my body reflexively convulsing and trembling. Its power was *un*fucking -believable!

Don's body spasmed so much and for so long, I grew concerned. I asked him if he was OK, which he was. He was just overcome by the magnitude of his climax and its aftershocks -- something he'd never gone through before.

Extending your love-making definitely produces the most amazing orgasms!

And it really deepens your feelings of love for each other -- and that's the very best part of it.

I mean, I still like quickies from time to time (our quickies, though are other lovers' *long*-ies). But if you really *love* your lover and you really *love* to make *love* to him or her...why *rush* it?

M.E.'s Story: Turning The Tables

I like turning the tables on my lover. You know, the man's supposed to be the dominant one, but I like switching roles. And, if the truth be told, I think my man likes it at least as much as I do.

I have to confess here to having a bit more experience than most women, in the ways of love. Without going into details, let's just say that I was always much in demand when I was in my 20s, for my expertise as a lover.

Now that I'm older and I'm no longer interested in being with anyone else but Jim, I'm finding that those skills come in REAL handy, so to speak, when it comes to keeping my man eager for more. (After all, you don't want your lover getting bored, do you?)

It's not like I don't enjoy it occasionally when Jim takes charge, but my pleasure is more akin to the violinist who gets her thrill from making the *violin* sing. I mean, the violin doesn't play the violinist, does it?

I know I'm different from some other women in that way, but, then again, there are plenty of men who would prefer it if their women took charge of the action in bed, like I do. While most men won't admit to it, I've found they quickly become submissive once I show them how much *fun* it can be!

Now, I don't know if you've read the book *The Proposal* or not, but that's the book that first opened my eyes to some of the more creative options a woman has in bed. I'd never heard of Ben Wa balls or anal beads or anything like that before I read that book. (That's the book that led to the movie Indecent Proposal. The book's a lot *hotter*, though. It's almost like a sex manual!)

Anyway, if you do your man right, he'll be like a puppy dog in your hands. He will never want another woman again -- if you give him something he can't get with anyone else.

One thing most women overlook is a man's *bottom*. The truth of the matter is that most men enjoy being fucked just as much as we women do. They might not realize it at first until you explore this end of things, so to speak. But, trust me. It absolutely knocks their socks off when you turn the tables on them!

I'll never forget the time I initiated Jim, so to speak, into this forbidden realm. He was already aware of my background (and he was tolerant of it although he wasn't too keen about it), and so I had tried to avoid some of the wild ways of my past so he wouldn't feel like I was acting like a professional, if you get my drift.

Well, one night, I decided, what the heck; let's get it on the way *I* like it!

So, I began by stripping him bare by the bedside while preventing him from touching me (I kept scolding him "Ah ah!" and pushing his hands away when he'd reach for my breasts or my pussy). Laying him down on the bed, I used a pair of my pantyhose to blindfold him and, in a very firm voice, I told him that *I* was in charge from then on -- that I was going to do to him whatever I wanted.

This was while I was securely tying his hands and feet to the bedposts, with two other sets of pantyhose.

I could see that being blindfolded and tied down got him VERY excited. His cock was stiffer than I'd ever seen it; the head was so engorged that it looked like it was absolutely going to explode! (I don't know why so few women seem to understand that most men, on occasion, want to be lovingly dominated, just as we do!)

Teasing his body with a feather, Jim was already writhing with pleasure. Looking at him, helpless, at my every whim, made me regret not having done this to him before.

Clear drops of fluid began to trickle out of the head of his penis as I ran circles around his belly with my fingers, never touching his genitals.

"Mmm," I said teasingly. "Somebody's getting really hot!"

Running my fingers down both of his thighs -- first down the tops of them, then down the sensitive inner sides -- his hard-on jerked spasmodically, although nothing came out.

"Oh, baby," he said pleadingly. "You're getting me too hot!"

"Ah ha," I said, running my hands down his legs,

making his back arch and his toes curl.

I was really getting wet as I saw the effect I was having on Jim, but I fought off the urge to mount him, and kept things nice and slow.

Turning my back to his face, I sat on his chest and leaned over to kiss the top of his feet. He started to moan and attempted to move in response, but I held him down firmly with my bottom, which only drove him madder!

Then, I sent his temperature skyrocketing by sucking all of his toes. He immediately began shouting "Oh!...Oh!...Oh!" as I really reamed each one, as if each one was a little cock. I kept this up for five or so minutes, his body gyrating more and more as my efforts grew more and more intense, until I suddenly stopped and sat up.

Placing my hands on each of his hips, I looked down and was pleased to see that Jim's hard-on had grown really, really red. Plus, I noticed that his belly now had pools of clear fluid, which had dripped from his cock. There's nothing more erotic than sweetly torturing your man in this way, and seeing the effects.

"Does my baby want to come?" I asked in a girlish voice.

"Yes," baby, he said. "PLEASE make me come!"

He was hotter than I'd ever seen him before!

"Not so soon, baby," I said, in my baby voice. "If you come I'm going to have to *spank* you!"

Turning around and lying down on his side, I began sucking on his nipples, rolling my tongue first around one, then the other, then nibbling them a little, then full-out sucking the shit out of them. Simultaneously, I started tickling his balls.

Jim was going *crazy!* He threw his head back, arching his back as though he was about to come, his breath growing real heavy (it sounded like he was gasping for air). His cries of *"Oh! Oh God!"* were growing louder and louder...

Again, I stopped abruptly.

"My baby really likes being dominated, don't you?" I teased.

He didn't answer, so I said: "Tell me you like being dominated, or I'll stop!"

"Yes, baby," he said, sounding hot and helpless. "I like it when you dominate me. Please don't stop," he begged.

"OK then," I responded, loving every moment.

Getting on top of him, I ran my breasts up and down his torso, which made him groan "mmmm." Every sound from him was like music to me.

Finally, sitting on his legs, I took his rampant

hard-on in one hand (firmly holding his shaft just below his cock head) and then I slowly ran circles around his balls with my tongue. His body began moving uncontrollably as I gently took one ball and then the other into my hot, wet mouth, sucking them lightly before running my tongue every which way over his scrotum. You'd think he was going to come, he was getting so turned on.

Again I put on the brakes.

"Oh, baby," I said, acting innocent. "You're so hot! Did I do something to make you so excited?"

"Yes," he panted, "you're torturing me with all this teasing! My cock's too hot!"

"Better cool down, buddy," I replied, again playing the dominatrix. "I don't want you coming right away when I put your big hard cock in my pussy!"

"Ohhh..." he said, the breath hissing from his lips as he responded to my mind fuck. When I got done teasing him, I knew that he was not going to last long in my pussy, and I think he knew it too. That was the point. That was my game of sweet humiliation.

Not letting him cool down, I turned my body around quickly so my back was again facing his face, and, taking his prick in my left hand, I used it to tease the outer lips of my pussy, shaking it quickly, several times up and down, with each motion, my pussy dripping wet (as was apparent from the squishing sound I made each time I ran his cock up and down the opening of my cunt).

"Oh, baby," Jim said. "You're going to make me come! I'm too hot"

"Not yet," I scolded, stopping altogether.

His cock WAS really hot! I could *feel* it! And the game I was playing *was* unfair, I admit, but I don't think he really minded it. It was driving him wild; I had never seen him so uncomfortably hot!

Taking his rock-hard penis in my hand again, I guided it between my pussy lips and slowly slid my hips down his body until he was in me to the max. It felt soooo good! (I forgot to tell you: Jim is hung like a horse!)

I just sat there, enjoying the feel of his throbbing cock, its heat, its stiffness, its size. Rapturous sensations were now coursing through my body, making me close my eyes and groan. My nipples were poking up like big, hard grapes.

"Oh," Jim said. "You're pussy feels like a *fire-place!* It's burning up!"

Turning my head around to give him a little taunting smile, I did not respond. I just began a rocking motion, grinding my hips on his hips at the downstroke, which silenced him. All he could do now was to groan. Is there anything more delicious?

His legs spread as wide as they could go (given the way I tied his feet to the bedposts), I reached over to the end table for the Vaseline I had placed there beforehand, taking a dab of it with two of my fingers.

"You see what I've got on my fingers, honey?" I said. "Someone's in for the fucking of their life!"

Straining his neck as if trying to see (but unable to, because of his blindfold), I heard him say only "Baby..." I gave him no time to react, immediately rubbing the vaseline up and down his crack with my fingers.

The effect was like placing a match to a furnace pilot light. You could almost hear the flames lighting up within Jim's body.

"Oh!...Oh God!" he screamed. "What are you doing to me?"

"I'm going to fuck you!" I replied. "Turnabout is fair play!"

"No, baby!...Oh!...Oh God!"

Although Jim had said "no," I could tell his body was saying: *yessss!*

Plunging my middle finger into his bottom, Jim went ballistic, shouting at the top of his lungs, suffering from the agony of sheer ecstacy.

"Oh! Oh! You're *fucking* me!" he said, clearly surprised that a woman could fuck a man. But, he was clearly loving it, too. (He wasn't getting angry with me at all.)

"Yes, I'm going to fuck you good, too!" I said, increasing the pace of my hip motion atop his cock.

Wiggling my fingers about 2 inches inside of Jim's bottom and feeling about the top wall, I had found his testicle-shaped prostate organ, and I began running wild circles on top of it until I had him going positively *crazy*. His anal muscles suddenly clamped down on my finger, his hips started fucking my fingers as if he was desperate to come, and I could tell it wouldn't be long now...

"Oh...baby!...baby!!!!!!!!!!!!!" Jim screamed, as I braced for his orgasm...which blew out of him like a shoulder-fired missile shooting out of its tube.

His cock throbbing and throbbing, an ocean of seed spurted into me, but I didn't stop. I began working toward my own climax, my hips going mad on top of Jim, my fingers now jerking up and down on my clit as quickly as I could, until an orgasm gripped me, in a huge wave of heat, goosebumps and spasms.

Collapsing to his right, we both lay there for what seemed hours, overwhelmed by the effects of our climaxes. I left Jim trussed up, though; I had something else in mind before I'd would let him go free.

"Oh," Jim finally said. "I've never come so hard...or so much!"

"You liked that, didn't you?" I teased.

"Yes," he said, sounding a bit embarrassed to admit it.

"Tell me you love it when I fuck you," I said.

"I love it when you fuck me," he said obediently.

That's when I was sure that he was getting off on being submissive, on being my sex slave, on being incapable of fighting off my sweet sexual torture, on being *taken*. Reaching over to the nightstand, I readied my next surprise.

Greasing up his bottom with some more vaseline, I grabbed one of the his-and-hers vibrating eggs I'd bought that day at the local adult toy store and began rubbing Jim's crack up and down with it.

"What are you doing now?" he said, tacitly

admitting both his sense of surprise and his willingness to surrender to his helplessness, in the tone of his voice.

"I'm going to fuck you again!" I said, popping the egg into his bottom.

"Ohhhhh!" he responded, as if shocked by how good it felt as well as by the novelty of what I was doing to him.

Turning the egg's vibrator on, Jim then dissolved into speechlessness, only able to moan from that point on, his cock swiftly rising to attention again, reignited with passion, as the vibrating egg made him delirious with incredible sensations I'm sure he'd never experienced before.

"You like that, don't you?" I said, but he could not respond, except with unintelligible groans.

Reaching over, I grabbed his growing cock and squeezed it hard while jerking it up and down, to bring it to a full erection. I was in need of having it inside me again.

Taking Jim's blindfold off (I wanted him to see what I was doing to him), I guided his now-stiff penis into my pussy, my butt firmly pressing down on his thighs. Leaning over his chest to French kiss him, I started rocking him again, this time feverishly rubbing my clit on his body, working toward my next orgasm.

I could feel the vibrations from the egg inside Jim through his cock, which made me hotter and more desperate to come. Stopping for a moment to grease up the other egg I'd bought with some vaseline, I shoved it inside my bottom and I, too, instantly grew crazed by the egg's sensations, no longer able to control myself.

Bouncing up and down violently now, Jim's cock iron-hard inside me, my clit starting to tingle, I was soon overcome by a positively *nuclear* climax, made all that more powerful when I felt Jim wriggling furiously and coming inside me at the same time.

My pussy kept throbbing and throbbing for minutes afterward, as little orgasmic aftershocks shook my body again and again.

As soon as I could, I untied Jim, and he passionately kissed me, up and down my body, as if he could not believe what I had done to him, while simultaneously expressing a sort of *gratitude,* and *love.* He obviously interpreted my taking him (correctly) as a very *loving* gesture. (Remember the old expression, "blow in his ear and he'll follow you anywhere"? I think this is what they might have been talking about!)

Since that night, I haven't hesitated to use some of my more exotic wiles on Jim. And I can tell, in his increased passion toward me, that it has helped bring us that much closer together as lovers.

And, that's what love is all about. Right?!

Don't tell me that the way to a man's heart is through his *stomach!*

H.D.'s Story: After Hours

I am not beyond influencing matters to my own ends, especially when it comes to sex.

Nor am I shy about satisfying my needs (which, unlike most other women I know, are *daily*). Such as it was when my boyfriend arrived at my place of business toward the end of a fragrant early Spring day. It was one of those days that stirs up your hormones and heightens your senses (where everything smells nice, and looks beautiful and your body tingles with the joys of being alive)...

With my senses vibrating with sensuality, it dawned on me that I could not afford to let Randy leave my office without getting him to attend to my awakened desires, or I'd go absolutely insane. So, I hatched a plan...

I asked him to stick around until the last of my employees had left, that I had something I wanted to show him. After the last worker had *finally* left for home, I invited him into the back office, unseen from the street.

We had been talking about a photographer friend of mine and the sensuous photos she'd taken of myself and my girlfriends, and I told him I wanted to show him her web site.

Clicking on the words "Sensuous Photography," the page I wanted him to see popped up on the computer screen. It was a gallery of naked women, all tastefully photographed, but, for chrissakes, they were nude, and I was hoping the photos would make Randy amorous.

"There's one I really want to show you," I told him, moving the cursor over to a photo of one of my friends, double-clicking on it to enlarge it.

"That's my friend Maria," I said, looking up at him to see his reaction. I saw his face flush a bit, and I thought *good, this is beginning to work.*

"Here; you sit down," I suggested, getting up from my desk chair and then setting him down in the chair, by the hips.

Looking up and down at Maria's curves, he expressed surprise at how big her breasts were.

"Yes, she kind of hides them under her clothes," I commented, pleased that the photo had captured his interest. He sat there for a few seconds admiring her curves, as I softly massaged the back of his neck.

He had only met Maria once, but I'd told him numerous stories about her, including the fact that she was intensely curious about his sexual prowess. She had surmised from my recent behavior that I was getting more than my share of great fucking (and she was *right,* but I didn't dish any details because I didn't want my girlfriends hitting on Randy).

I should tell you that, knowing beforehand that my boyfriend would be coming to my store that afternoon to drop something off, I'd purposely worn one of my sexiest outfits to work. I had on my black fishnet stockings (held up with black garter belts), sexy strappy stiletto-heeled shoes, a velvety black skirt (with *no* panties on underneath it), and a red V-neck lightweight sweater, which revealed one of my best attributes, my ample cleavage. (He definitely took notice of my clothes upon catching his first glimpse of me that evening. He immediately told me: "You look very pretty!" And I thought: *Yesss! I've got him!*)

Leaning across him provocatively (my breasts strategically placed near his face, so he could feel the body heat rising off them, and get a whiff of my enchanting perfume), I grabbed the mouse with my left hand and clicked on the word NEXT.

"You might like the next photo even better!" I said in my most seductive voice.

It was of me. I saw his eyes grow wide momentarily, as the image loaded onto the screen. There I was, totally bare, sitting on my heels, my face demurely turned away, my arms above my head, showing off my alabaster skin and my breathtaking (if I do have to say so myself) C-cup breasts.

"That one's great," he said, in a deep bedroom voice, sounding like it came on a wave of testosterone.

"Yes," I said, "but do you know what I'd really like? I'd love her to take a photo of you! You wouldn't have to be nude, although that would be nice. You could have a pair of jeans on, but that's all! No undies, nothing else!"

He turned his chair in my direction and took a deep breath, his nostrils flaring. Not missing a beat, I reached down to his waist and grabbed the bottom of his black chenille sweater, deftly denuding him of it in one quick motion. Then, I knelt down to his feet and removed his black boots and socks.

"There!" I said. "That's how I like you best!"

I had done my job well. I walked right up to Randy (who was still seated in my office chair) and he pulled me toward him in a bear hug, giving me a French kiss with such emotion and power that he made me a bit weak, and I needed to lie down on the floor.

"No," he said, his virile hands stopping me from completing my swoon to the floor.

Skillfully popping open the hooks of my bra with his left hand, Randy whipped off my bra and top in one adept move. I went from being clothed to being topless in less than 5 seconds.

He then took my breath away as his experienced hands stole up the back of my skirt, caressing the backs of my knees and then my inner thighs. It wasn't long before I felt his magical fingers stretching my pussy lips open wide.

"Oh," I groaned, feeling myself growing even weaker. I wanted to succumb to the feeling and fall to the floor, but when I tried, he used his arms to hold my thighs and tummy tight to his chest.

"No! You'll have to *stand* for this," he intoned.

My body held against his, as if chained there, his fingers explored my inner wetness, and then used it to massage my protruding pussy lips. At the same time, still seated, he surrounded my right nipple with his wonderful lips and sucked it with such strength I thought I was going to come right there. His tongue began giving my stone-hard nipple a rhythmic massage as his fingers took up the same rhythm, going back and forth along the inside of the inch or so of lippy flesh sticking out of my pussy.

The feeling of being a virtual prisoner, of wanting -- no, of *needing* to faint to the floor, but being *prevented* from doing so by his strong arms encircling my body, made the sensual onslaught that much more arousing. I did try to fight off his arms, but I was frustrated in my efforts by his iron grip around me. I couldn't have gotten away from him had I used every resource available to me. That made me soooooo hot!

I thought all of this would lead to wild sex, but he continued his sweet tormenting, pushing all of my buttons. The visual image of him sitting there with his muscular bare chest, bulging arms and bare feet raised my internal temperature even higher, the blue shade of his faded jeans nicely accentuating the hue of his skin.

And then...all of this took on a greater urgency, as I felt some serious tingling growing in my pussy, my clit, my tits and within my ass canal. His fingers and nipple sucking was growing more insistent. He had increased the rhythm and power of his erotic massage...It didn't take very long before I began screaming as I felt myself melting away in a climax that seemed to shake the very ground I stood on.

My body collapsed in his arms, nicely spent.

"That was nice," he said, in velvety-soft baritone tones.

Swinging his chair around while holding my hips, he sat me down on my office desk. I was still bleary-eyed from my orgasm, but, in lifting my skirt above my waist and guiding my bare bottom onto the cool desktop, my feet (still in my stilettos) dangling off the ground, he had created in me new desires, the *need* for more sexual attention and release. (It felt peculiarly exciting to feel the coolness of my desk on my skin!)

The pose he'd put me in was also new to me, causing my head to feel like it was spinning, a whole new wave of heat spreading, like wildfire, up from my thighs all the way to my brain. Spreading my legs, he pulled my bottom toward him while pushing my top softly backward so that I had to lean back on the wall.

(From the corner of my eyes, I could see that my nude picture was still on the computer screen, and seeing it somehow made me hotter, as if I was telescoping time to see the consequences of my nude modeling. At the time I had posed for the picture, I was imagining that I was lighting a fire under the men who would later see it, and here I was, being fucked by one of those men!)

My moist cunt was now inches from his face, exposed to his every desire, and he wasted no time in burying his head between my legs. His talented hot tongue was like a laser-guided missile, finding its mark in seconds -- the little marble that now swelled outside of its hood at the top of my slit.

I felt his fingers spreading my pussy lips apart in

order to better tease my clit with his darting tongue. With a light touch, he began an irresistible up and down rhythmic licking motion going no further than the top and bottom of my clitoris. He kept this up until, in a matter of seconds, I reached my second climax.

"Oh, so fast, so fast!" I heard myself panting. "You made me come so fast! I think I'm disappointing you!"

"No, I like it that way," he cooed.

"Hey," he added. "I *love* making you come. And, I'm not done with you yet!"

And, with that, he plunged his tongue back between my legs. Knowing he had my number, he repeated *exactly the same great tonguing he'd just given me before.* I came even faster than the first time.

I actually had to *peel* his lips *away* from my pussy after my rapture had peaked, because the pleasure of his tongue laving my clit was so intense that it was approaching the painful stage.

My eyes closed, attempting to regain my equilibrium, I felt Randy getting up from the chair, and then I heard him unbuckling his belt, unzipping his jeans, and pulling his pants off. I then managed, with some difficulty, to break the heavy spell cast

on me by my condition and open my eyes, to see
him delicately raising the top of his underwear
over the head of his bulging cock in order to pull it
off without hurting himself.

The engorged head of his penis was already
dripping. He cock was enormous. The sight of it
made me breathless.

Sliding me off the desk with his strong hands, he
now turned me around so I was standing up,
facing the desk. Pushing my head down so I was
bent over, resting on my arms on the desktop, he
raised my skirt above my waist to bare my privates
and my bottom for whatever he chose to do next.

Pressing down forcefully on my back with his
right hand so I could not move, I looked backward
as best as I could. I saw him take his rampant
penis in his left hand, and then I felt him putting
his cock between my legs, guiding the *back* of his
rod so that it covered the span of my cleft.

Rubbing the back of his shaft back and forth
along my pussy lips in a gentle rocking motion for
what seemed like five minutes or more, he got me
good and hot...and then he stopped just as I
thought I was about to climax! Teasingly removing
his cock when he knew I needed it most, he then
returned its head to the lips of my entrance and

gradually insinuated its entire length into my pussy.

"Oh God!" I cried out.

I felt as if I had become just about as hot as I could have gotten, but this insertion sent my level of excitement soaring. And just as I thought I'd reached the peak again, he began fucking me in earnest, removing the *entire* length of his cock so that its head was perched at my very entrance, and then rapidly slipping it all the way inside, in a regular motion, over and over.

"Oh, I'm burning up!" I confessed.

I'm a freak about wanting my lover to give me the feeling of being taken, so when I felt his left hand move up to grab my hair to hold my head lovingly but firmly down on the desktop, that turned the flames up on me. And that, combined with the feeling of being fucked, half-dressed, from behind, brought on a withering weakness, the love-making stimulation reaching so critical a stage that I knew my climax was now inevitable, coming on like a hand slowly clenching.

"Oh...oh...you're going to make me come!" I said, thrilling in the fact that I had no control over this, that he had done something to *make* me lose it, like the hand that squeezes every drop of juice from an orange.

Upon hearing my admission, he notched up the speed and ferocity of his sweet assault, while running the nails of his hands over my spine and the backs of my thighs (sending shivers up and down my back) until I was yelling at the top of my lungs: "Oh God!!!! Oh God, oh God, oh God!" -- the fact that I was coming atop my office desk, making it that much more trippy.

Temporarily incapacitated by my ravishment, Randy slowed down to reduce my internal flames to a simmer, and then did something that was astonishing and absolutely fabulous. Placing the middle finger of his right hand onto the crack of my ass, he began to rub it tantalizingly up and down...and then...he used that finger and *entered* my bottom! No one had ever done that to me before!

It felt as if I had two cocks, two men inside of me -- absolutely blowing my mind (having two men doing me at the same time is one of my fantasies). I never told Randy, but my mind instantly fantasized that his finger wasn't a finger, but another man's penis.

Working his hard-on inside my cunt with renewed vigor while slowly penetrating my ass until his long, lovely finger was in as far as it was going to go and was wiggling deep inside my anus, I knew right away that I wouldn't last too long. The double stimulation was creating an unfamiliar but powerful, tingling feeling in my butt as Randy's cock stroked my G Spot into a ball of tension that was going to burst any moment...and that moment was...NOW!

Sending me into a furious, multicolored orgasm, I screamed multiple times as I came in a *flood* of juices, my arms flailing, my body rippling with convulsions, and then the aftershocks of my climax, for what seemed like several minutes, enhanced by the fact that Randy was *not* stopping!

Now moving his bottom-lodged finger in circles as his cock began to pound my pussy, he then grabbed a hold of either side of my clit with the thumb and forefinger of his other hand, shaking it violently and rhythmically until I felt myself tensing up again...

"Randy!" I panted. "You're going to make me...make me come...again!"

And I came again -- within a few minutes of my last orgasm!

Gasping for breath, I begged Randy to let me rest. I was *shaking* all over.

Covering my heaving body with his hot, sweaty torso, Randy held me for awhile as I melted away in a state of ecstacy. I felt like my *soul* was floating far above the Earth, somewhere in the heavens.

...And now...you might not believe this, but he wasn't through with me!

As soon as he felt I had recuperated enough, Randy took me by the hand and instructed me to remove my shoes and lay facedown *on the floor of my office.* I was like a limp rag doll at this point, so I didn't feel I had the strength to object. Lying down as he'd instructed, the inexpensive office carpet felt a bit rough on my skin, but not altogether unpleasant.

Randy, knowing my favorite thing was being taken from behind, he again entered me in that way, but in a very unusual way he'd never done before -- by balancing on the balls of his feet, which were now on either side of my buttocks. (The rear-entry position is great because his penis really engages my G Spot.)

With a combination of bouncing and rocking, he plunged his stiff into me with wild abandon -- just as I liked it -- and my overheated body gave way to Randy's masterful cocking in no time at all. To my own disbelief, it only took a minute or so before I was coming once again, in a deluge of hot cum.

Now moving his feet forward so he could lean back and steady himself by holding my feet (which is a hot position because it feels kind of like you've been shackled to the floor), he rocked back and forth, back and forth until, in spite of feeling I was already spent, I quickly found myself in the throes of yet another orgasm!

I couldn't take anymore -- I was shaking and throbbing all over. So, gathering what little energy I had left, I managed to unencumber myself from my compromising position, and grab onto his wet, steaming hot cock so that I could turn the tables on him.

Guiding him by the cock back to the chair, I spread his legs and knelt between them, placing my head on his as I regained my composure, while I jerked on his hard-on with one hand.

My breath settling down, I raised my head and greedily swallowed five or six inches of him, the sight of his colossal hard-on making my blood run hot. Tasting my own juices and catching the fragrance of my own pussy on his cock turned me on, as I took the head of his penis in my mouth and went absolutely *wild* on him.

Cupping his balls in my right hand, and earnestly working up and down his shaft with my left, I sucked him hard until I felt his body tense after a few minutes.

Pausing a moment for a tease, I looked up and said, "Well, sailor, it looks like you're about to blow out some steam!"

Moaning and weakened by my words, I returned to reaming Randy and, to my pleasure, it took me just *seconds* to make him come in huge spurts. With Randy emitting a scream I thought might have been heard next door (I wondered what they might have thought!), I enthusiastically drank down all of his salty liquor, savoring every drop.

Cuddling me to his chest and kissing me repeatedly all over my face -- my eyes, cheeks and mouth -- I knew then and there he was *the* lover for me. He'd made me really happy in the days and weeks I'd known him.

Helping me up, we held each other for what seemed like hours. Feeling his wet, semi-hard cock against my tummy, his bare skin against mine, the love was welling up in my heart. I couldn't hold him close enough!

With one final kiss, Randy lovingly helped me on with my clothes, brushing my hair into place, and then he took me out to a nice dinner at a *very* romantic restaurant. We held hands most of the meal, and I had my hand on his thigh when we didn't, right near his glorious cock. (I could see the bulge in his pants swell up a bit whenever I did so, which got me hot all over again!)

Once we were back home, Randy drew the water in the bathtub and bathed me in scented water, the tub surrounded by candles. He then tenderly dried me off, and took me to bed, tucking me in before going downstairs to shut the house down.

Already half adrift in sleep, I felt Randy slip under the covers and spoon with me, his arms wrapped around me, my hands holding his. And then we both drifted off into a wonderfully deep slumber, under the glowing aura of love.

As you can imagine, from that time on, it's been difficult for me to sit at my office desk without reliving the whole sexy scenario over again in my mind...In fact, there's still a vague scent of my pussy lingering on the desk, which gives me quivers as I remember how Randy ate me out...

So, many's the day I now feel wetness growing between my legs, along with the anticipation and hope that Randy might surprise me -- right then --

and return to do me again, the way he'd done me that one incredible night.

But, so far, he's made me wait, knowing full well how *much* I need another office fucking! How do you like that?

It's not fair! (But he *knows* what he's doing, by getting me so worked up about it, doesn't he?!)

It sure does keep things interesting, though. (And the anticipation sure helps to make my work day fly by quicker!).

K.C.'s Story: Makeup Sex

Kenn and I had had a bad tiff on the plane ride home after visiting with his parents in New York and we hadn't spoken to each other since then.

We had been together for nearly a year by that time, and, although we had had one brief separation before, we had since grown quite close and I was truly in love with him.

So, naturally I was devastated by this latest turn of events. My days were hours of frazzled nerves and loneliness, and my nights were no better. I was so used to snuggling up to Kenn in bed that I couldn't sleep at night without his warm body next to mine.

I was hoping he'd call, but three days had gone by since we'd parted in a bad way at the airport and I was heartbroken that I hadn't heard from him since. Enough time had gone by, I thought; too much. So I summoned all the courage I could and phoned him.

"Hi," I ventured, "I've missed you."

"Hi," Kenn replied.

"I'd really like to get together and talk with you, if you want to," I continued.

"OK, if you want to," Kenn said, not giving me much encouragement. He'd felt I'd been very critical of him the last time we were together, and he still sounded annoyed.

"I think I know what our problem is," I said.

"What's that?" he asked.

"I think we have a communication problem."

"Really?"

Kenn sounded skeptical but he agreed to meet me for a talk. I arrived at his house the next night after he'd returned from his men's group meeting. It was nearly 10 o'clock and both of us were tired, but I was determined to turn things around. To be honest, I was intent on having hot makeup sex.

I was dressed in one of my sexiest dresses, a slinky, low-cut red number with a slit practically up to my hip, with NO panties and NO bra. On my feet I wore strappy wedges that screamed "fuck me!"

I hoped that Kenn would rip off my dress as soon as I entered his house, but I was disappointed to find that he was acting a bit grumpy, although he did look sexy in his faded jeans, tight black tee shirt and bare feet.

"Are you going to make me a drink?" I asked, in my best come-on voice.

"Sure," he said, "what would you like?"

"Make me a Brandy Alexander," I replied, playing a sultry Lauren Bacall (like she was in Key Largo), sashaying into Kenn's living room, and settling onto Kenn's couch.

Quickly whipping my drink together, Kenn joined me on the couch, but he started wiping his eyes as if he was bushed.

"OK…so what did you want to talk about?" he asked wearily.

"Maybe you're too tired to talk," I cooed. I was being hopeful. I was the one who didn't want to talk.

I crossed my legs and casually let my dress fall back so my thighs were provocatively exposed. Moving up close to Kenn, I took his left hand and directed his arm so it surrounded me, his hand resting on my bare hip, exposed through the slit in my dress.

Sipping on my drink and smiling coyly at Kenn, I noticed his hand beginning to move…first exploring my bare hip, then the V between the top of my thigh and my tummy. His middle finger now traced that V all the way down to where it met my bush, then back to my hip. The effect was electric; I had goosebumps on my hips, butt and tummy. I decided to lose my drink and take matters into my hands.

…Actually…I'm going to tell you this story…a story of how I won Kenn back, but, sadly, before I finished writing this story, I fucked up our relationship…I did some things that I should never have done, and I'm not sure Kenn will ever forgive me (I'm not sure I'd forgive myself, if the shoe had been on the other foot).

So, what I'd like to do is to dedicate this story to Kenn, so maybe he'll read it and see what he meant to me, and just maybe I won't lose the best man I've ever loved. Because – and I used to joke with him about this – once you've been loved by Kenn, you're spoiled; no one else will do. (I used to tell him, "Your poor ex's – they'll never be able to be with another man again!")

It's not just that he has the biggest cock I've ever seen. That was, of course, great. But, what makes Kenn a great lover is the fact that he is a lover 24/7. A *giving* lover. And I should never have done anything to risk losing him. I was a damn fool.

Kenn could get me wet during the day simply by touching me. Or talking to me. It was the damndest thing.

He has the greatest hands. Long, long fingers… When he touched me, it would strike a chord deep inside me. When he'd make love to me, those hands would be all over me, playing me like a harp. He'd touch places I'd never been touched before.

And – no matter how long we'd been together (we were together 10 months when he broke up with me) – he'd always surprise me in bed. Every time was different. And there was always at least one major surprise or two. One of my friends, Jerry, would always say to me: "Is it boring yet? The newness will wear off and it'll becoming boring. It always does." But she was wrong, although she never believed me when I told her how good a lover Kenn was. Few women experience that kind of lovemaking – even once in a lifetime — so I don't blame Jerry for being cynical. I was cynical in that way before I met Kenn.

No man could ever keep up with me until I met Kenn. I wore the others out. I mean that literally. I physically wore them down by my sexual appetite, which is huge. Not Kenn. He not only could keep up with me, he regularly wore ME out! Once, twice, three, four or more times a day, Kenn was right there for me, and I was the one begging Kenn to stop. When Kenn would get done with me, I was on the verge of passing out, of blacking out. Often, I was so dizzy, I couldn't stand up.

Anyway, let me go back to telling you about the last time we were together…we were on the couch and I was trying to induce Kenn, who was annoyed with me, to indulge in some make-up sex.

Placing my glass on the table to my left, I leaned over, resting my head on Kenn's chest, my left hand exploring his inner thighs, and then rubbing directly over the growing bulge in his jeans.

"Mmm!" he said, closing his eyes. I knew then that things were going in my direction. He was giving in to my lead.

So, always the impatient one, I got up and removed his belt, undid his jeans button and unzipped his zipper in a hurry – not terribly smooth about it, I admit (I fumbled with his button), but I was in a rush. Both of us laughed as I grabbed the ends of his pants legs and tugged his jeans off – I just about fell on my ass when they came off!

Kenn offered no resistance, either, as I grabbed the tops of his briefs and whipped those off too. His dick was already stiff and I eagerly got on my knees and gobbled it down.

Coming up for air, I paused to marvel: "Are you bigger than ever? You ARE!" He was enormous, amazing.

Finally throwing himself into it, he maneuvered the cocktail table I was kneeling next to so that it was out of our way, and then got down on the floor with me, pushing me on my back, and my feet (still in my shoes), over my head.

And, this is what made him such an unusually fantastic lover – his hands were all over me, igniting all my sensitive areas (many of which I didn't even know I had!), and, as he began giving me head – my feet still over my head – he was so tender about it. He started by kissing my vulva, up and down, as if he was smooching my lips. Every brush of his lips or his tongue said *I love you!*

That night, for the first time ever, once he'd spent minutes setting my pussy on fire, I suddenly felt his tongue thrusting deeply up my hole until it was right over my G Spot! I couldn't believe it! No one had done that before! But he was always surprising me.

Holding the backs of my thighs tightly in place, my tongue-ravaged body fighting his efforts to hold me still, he kept his tongue deep inside me, right on my G Spot, tickling it furiously, nonstop, until Superman couldn't have held me down. My legs were flying, my arms, my body jumping up and down as he sent me off on a rip-roaring climax no woman could have sat still for. I was grabbing my head at the end, groaning, rocking back and forth, wondering *what just hit me?* I was hit by a *Mac truck!*

Pulling me up to a sitting position, he gave me one of those post-head, pussy-musk-scented passionate French kisses he was great for, which only made me want more, of course.

Helping me onto my feet (I wasn't very steady at the moment), he led me by the hand, around the room, past the piano, and I thought we were heading upstairs to his bedroom, but he instead placed me over the back of the couch, standing up, leaning over, my dress up over my back, my bare bottom and legs exposed to him, my shoes still on. Placing the head of his cock on my slit, his legs on either side of mine, he started shaking it up and down, shake-shake-shake (pause), shake-shake-shake (pause), the head just inside my vulva. Reaching back with my hands and pushing back with my hips, I sucked his cock into my hungry pussy, pulling on his hips to set up a quick rhythm – I needed to be *fucked* as only he knew how to do it!

I can't properly describe what he did to me at that point…all I can say is that when he was done with me, I had come three or four times, and I was finally thrown over the couch with his final thrusts, my body no longer able to resist his powerful forward momentum. Like a boxer TKO'd, I lay there limp, whimpering *oh! oh! oh!,* facedown, breathless, half on the couch, half on the floor, in need of recovery time.

When I was finally able to, I struggled with some difficultly to get my whole body onto the couch. Kenn, still hard as a rock (and he hadn't come yet, mind you), wandered over to my side, laying his head next to mine, solicitous of my condition.

"Are you OK, baby?" he asked.

"Yeah…" I said, still laboring to breathe, as if I'd just run a marathon. "You only split me in two!"

Laughing, he stayed with me for a good while, snuggling with me as best he could, until I was finally strong enough to get up and make it up the stairs to his bedroom. Pulling off my dress and removing my shoes, I looked at Kenn looking at me and said, "Get over here!"

Throwing my arms around his neck, we kissed as if it was our first French kiss, the feeling of having his warm, naked body pressed against mine, heavenly. Feeling kittenish, I threw myself back on the bed, pulling Kenn along with me, both of us laughing as we bounced up and down on the mattress.

Locked in a kiss again, I directed Kenn's body so it was over mine, his legs on either side of mine, and guided his massive cock so its head was right up against my pussy lips. I wanted more!

But Kenn, always a teaser, always thinking of something new, would only give me an inch or two of his cock, and wouldn't move it at all – he just kept kissing me, which was really sexy, and was getting me incredibly hot!

Desperately needing him to fill me up and do me, I tried hard to pull his butt to move him in deeper, but he was stronger than me and, playing coy, he refused to budge. He just kept kissing me, feverishly, with the hottest tongue action you can imagine.

It was too much. I started grinding my hips on his cock, what little he'd allowed me to have, practically pleading with him to fuck me, but he was intent on teasing me.

So, I had to do myself! Reaching down with my right hand (Kenn gave it room enough to reach my clit), I started to masturbate.

"That's right, baby," he cooed. "Show me how hot I've made you!"

He allowed me another inch or so of his hard-on, enough to grind my hips on, but he stayed motionless, impaling me on his hot, hard cock while I rapidly jerked myself into a state of delirium.

Reaching down with his left hand, his fingers dipping into my pussy for some honey, he raised that hand up to my lips, rubbing my wetness all over them.

"Taste my fingers, baby," he said, slipping them

into my mouth, where I hungrily sucked on them. The thought of what he was making me do was ...it was the sexiest thing anyone had ever done to me.

"Can you taste yourself?" he added, and I excitedly nodded yes, as I felt him slip another inch or so of his hard-on into me, which only made me hornier.

Passionately kissing me again while leaving me impaled on his cock without relief, he drove me crazy again with desire, until I was again thrashing my hips about and, finally, taking matters into my own hands again.

"That's right, baby, masturbate for me," he said, in his sweet, deep, breathy bedroom voice. "Show me how hot my cock makes you!"

And I did! And it felt downright nasty...but really nice! Sucking madly on one of my tits as I approached my climax, he then pushed his cock in as far as it would go and held it there just as I came, notching everything up to a higher level, making my climax reach gigantic proportions.

Kenn had now shoved his enormous cock past the length of my vagina walls, into my cervix, and he began rocking back and forth just an inch or so, back and forth, until I started getting a feeling like a tight ball of energy was building up there. Kissing me with great passion again, I felt his left hand exploring my pussy lips, gently stretching them like no one had ever done before. Sloppy wet now, his wide cock stretching me to the limit, stimulating my inner reaches no one's reached before...I could feel another orgasm coming on, and I think Kenn sensed it, because his fingers were now rapidly thrashing at the flesh at the bottom V of my vagina, and suddenly, suddenly, it sent a huge tingle through me and...I blasted off...and practically blacked out!

I got kind of scared, actually...my heart was palpitating heavily, I was having trouble breathing, my head was reeling...

"OK, OK!" I said, holding Kenn's body still.

"Are you all right, honey?" he asked, worried.

"I'm just...dizzy!" I said, holding my head.

Pulling himself out of me, and lying to my side, Kenn held me and rocked me, and spoke to me soothingly, until I calmed down from my overexcited state.

"Whew!" I said, when I had gotten over my scare, and was certain I was going to live. "No one's ever done that to me before!"

And they hadn't. And that's why I'm so upset I

loused everything up later on. I've tried calling him several times, but he's told me "It's over, Kathy," and I still can't believe it is. I don't want it to be.

Our lovemaking was too great to let it come to an end. I can see why most of his ex's are still calling him, asking him to come back. And, unfortunately, I've become one of them.

L.L.'s Story: The Very First Night

I want to tell you about the first night I went out on a date with Rick.

Because, what happened that night was so unexpected and *so romantic*.

A mutual friend of ours, Ed, had set us up. We had first met months before, at a party Ed and his wife had thrown, but both of us were entangled in other relationships at the time, so nothing came of it.

But I think it would be fair to say that we were both flirting with each other at Ed's party. In fact, it's always been my contention that Rick was actually coming on to me, although he'll tell you that he was just fooling around.

I had gone to that party dressed in a very provocative outfit. I was wearing a tight, extremely low-cut black dress, which showed off my nicely rounded breasts in such a blatant way that I could see that everyone -- men and women -- were a bit embarrassed and yet a bit turned on when I'd walk over to say hello.

A woman can tell such things. I could see a faint blush come across their faces. Then, they'd smile a bit too much, and act warmer to me than they'd ever been.

Rick was no exception (although he wasn't so put off by my bold attire; it didn't make him act shy or silly). Another difference with Rick was that he cut a very striking figure and I was aware of being sexually attracted to him (yet I was also *afraid* of him at the same time -- he seemed so self-assured and, perhaps, a bit *cocky,* as if he was no stranger to women).

Anyway, Ed's party was a lot of fun. We were all assigned a partner to cook with, and given instructions as to how we should participate in making the night's meal together, which was risotto.

I was, fortunately, paired up with *Rick*, by Ed's wife Dee. The chemistry between us was unmistakable from the start. It felt to me as if we were bathing each other in seductive waves of nose-opening pherormones and body heat. Standing so near to Rick, I noticed that my breathing had become slower and deeper.

However, our fun came and went with the party. We both had lovers to return home to (although neither of us was aware that both of us were unhappy in those relationships).

Months later, once we independently had broken up with our prospective lovers, Ed began a very clever campaign to get us together, unbeknownst to Rick and me. Ed, ever the good friend, felt we'd be good for each other.

For weeks, Ed told Rick that I had expressed an interest in him (not true) and that Rick would be crazy not to ask me out. Ed told me the same thing about Rick -- that he had requested my phone number (not true) and that he desperately wanted to go out with me.

Finally, after so much friendly badgering, Rick broke down and phoned me, on a Friday afternoon, inviting me to meet him at a local pub for drinks. I gladly accepted his offer. (That meant breaking off a previous date with someone else, but I didn't say anything to Rick about that.)

Actually, as I recall, I was a bit *annoyed* at Rick for asking me out for THAT night. I thought it was a bit *presumptuous.* (Did he think I had no one else to go out with, or that I'd drop everything for him?) I was also a bit aggravated at him when I tried to put him off until the following night, but he suggested that he couldn't because he had *plans.*

That notwithstanding, his deep, sexy voice had immediately gotten me going on the phone, and so I found myself unable to say no to his proposition.

I should tell you, too, that Ed had hinted to me that Rick was quite accomplished as a lover. And, the inference was that he was also well *hung --* and therefore much in demand by women. So, that had aroused my curiosity, to say the least.

I arrived a bit late to our first rendezvous and Rick was already at the nicely appointed bar by the time I stumbled in (I literally *tripped*, to my embarrassment, when I saw how *gorgeous* Rick looked that night, dressed to the 9s). But Rick seemed unperturbed by my tardiness and my clumsiness.

Flashing a beautiful smile and enveloping my right hand in his large, masculine hands in a warm greeting, I could feel goosebumps spreading from my nipples, to my breasts, to my arms -- all over my body. I could feel my temperature rising, too, my body heat rising off my breasts and brushing by my blushing face.

I had to draw a deep breath. I already *wanted* him...and *badly*.

He was stunning, dressed like a GQ man, with a velvety black shirt, mauve pleated microwoven pants, and stylish hightop black shoes, and I felt myself getting a little intoxicated from the scent of his marvelous cologne. I wanted him to hug me tight and kiss me right then and there!

It didn't surprise me when I felt myself getting moist between my legs only seconds after I'd sat down on the barstool next to him. I couldn't help but smile and gaze into his lovely eyes. It didn't matter what he said from then on; I was already hooked!

My throat felt tight and thoughts and words eluded me, but I'm not sure Rick noticed how much trouble I was having in conversing with him. I was so overtaken by my emotions I could barely think anything but: *let's do it...now!*

One of the first things I noticed were his long, virile fingers. I imagined what they would feel like cupping my breasts, and then touching me all over -- inside and out! I don't know why I instinctively *knew* they were *talented* hands, but I had the impression that they knew how to work a woman over, how to caress her tantalizingly, how to make her juices come down...how to *satisfy* her.

The sight of Rick's large hands also took my breath away because I couldn't help but wonder if the supposed correlation held true -- that a man's *penis* size is in direct proportion to the length of his fingers. I was hoping Rick didn't pick up on my thoughts as his eyes seemed to look directly into my soul, and he smiled a knowing smile.

"You have beautiful hands," I told him. "Has any woman told you that before?"

"Mmm hmmm," he acknowledged, still smiling his sexy, confident smile, the bass tones of his voice causing something to vibrate deeply inside of me.

I took one of his hands in mine, turning it over and running one of my manicured nails over the lines of his palm. I thought I noticed his eyes dilate a bit in response.

The bartender interrupted us, unfortunately, and so the mood was broken for a bit as we ordered (he had a seven and seven; I had my usual dirty martini). But, once the drinks were served, the conversation again was extremely stimulating -- even though I don't quite *remember* the details.

It wasn't the alcohol we drank that led to my amnesia about the topics we covered. My forgetfulness was more likely the result of some kind of hormonal high, from my overheated state. To me, the time we spent together at that pub on our first date resides in my memory as just a wonderful haze. I can tell you that we were there for at least two to three hours before the check came (which Rick graciously paid, along with a generous tip). We then both rose from our barstools as if led by fate to our next destination.

When we'd gotten to the parking lot, Rick asked me if I wanted to go to a nightclub or somewhere else but, to my own surprise, I suggested instead that perhaps he'd like to come to my house "for some tea."

"Sure, that sounds good," he said, causing tingles of excitement to traverse my face, down to my nipples, tummy, hips and thighs.

Afraid he might change his mind, I turned and

ran to my SUV and then breathlessly drove home,
with Rick following closely behind me. Part of me
was thinking *what am I doing, I've just met the guy
and I'm taking him home?!* But I was driven by an
uncontrollable urge to jump his bones and I was
unable to fight off that impulse! He looked too
yummy, and there was no way I was going to let
him get away from me that night.

I don't remember Rick drinking much of the tea I
served him. I do remember excusing myself and,
feeling wonderfully naughty, I took off my bra and
pantyhose in my bathroom (and I wasn't wearing
any undies), which left my shapely legs and pussy
totally bare.

I set up this ruse almost autonomically. I felt I
had no choice but to seduce Rick. I was pulling
out all the stops, like an automaton who absolutely
needed sexual satisfaction, who would do almost
anything to accomplish that end.

Flushing the toilet to cover up my real intentions,
I rejoined Rick and led him to the hot red loveseat
I'd just bought for my livingroom. Slipping off my
strappy wedges and sitting down sideways, I
placed my bare feet *under* his right thigh. That's
right! Boy, was I bad! Not only that -- my knees
were bent and my dress strategically raised a bit to

give him a good look at the bottoms of my bare thighs (and maybe, I wasn't sure, a glimpse of my pussy).

I was very proud to see that my little plan worked immediately. Rick turned sideways and leaned toward me a bit, looking in my eyes as if trying to verify what he was reading from my body language. Almost absentmindedly, however, he took my bare feet in his warm hands, which then led him to caress my calves and then the insides of my thighs, which, as you might imagine, made me so hot and bothered I was now beyond the point of no return. (Rick later told me that he suspected I was wearing nothing under my dress and it was driving him wild!)

...All the while he was exciting every nerve in my body, he kept talking to me about something that had nothing to do with sex...But I wasn't really listening and he didn't seem to mind when I interrupted him and said: "Would you like to come upstairs and spend the night?"

For a second, he hesitated. I think the offer came as a bit of a shock. I could tell he was briefly debating the wisdom of having sex on the first date, but, tilting his head a bit, his eyes smiling in a sexy way, he responded: "I would *love* to!"

A thought then flew through my mind...*hey, I don't know this guy...this could be dangerous...* But I honestly *couldn't help myself!* I needed his cock and I needed it *now!*

I instantly removed Rick's shoes and socks and then, getting up from the couch, I took him by the hand and led him up the winding wood staircase to my room -- all the while *stripping* him. I worked his shirt buttons open and then the zipper on his pants before we'd reached the first landing. I had his shirt off on the lower part of the staircase, his pants on the top; by the time we were standing at my bedside, his clothes littered the path to my bed.

Practically throwing him on top of the bed, I whipped off my dress and jumped on top of him, giving him a big, wet kiss while my hand found its way to his cock, already standing stiff inside his briefs. I was not disappointed. The rumors were *true*. Ed had not lied to me.

Rick's cock was so long that the head of his penis *was poking out of the top of his undies!* He was so *thick* around that I heard myself stop and say "Rick! You are a *big* man!"

"Mm hmm!" he acknowledged in his velvety voice, letting go a little laugh, and then flashing me a sexy smile full of promise.

Furiously kissing him now, I pulled down his underwear and grabbed his hard-on, jerking it up and down frantically as I lost total control of myself. His lips were luscious, and he was a *great* kisser. The feel of his tongue making circles around my lips and then darting into my mouth in shallow explorations made my blood boil and my pussy gush with juices.

The scent of his cologne and the feel of his skin next to mine...it was too much! I pulled him on top of me, and, grabbing his gigantic hard-on, I directed his cock into my dripping cunt.

Easing his huge member into my pussy, I felt my inner walls being stretched wide like they'd never been stretched before. I came, screaming, before he'd even inched his way in all the way!

"Cockadoodle doo!!!!" I screamed (I don't know why, but I've always said "cockadoodle doo!" when I've had a great orgasm!).

I was laughing, crying...*this was the man I had dreamed about all my life!*

Placing my hands on his nice bottom, I physically encouraged him to start fucking me. One orgasm wasn't nearly enough. Not tonight. Not with this man.

I wasn't disappointed as he started to rock back and forth, pulling his cock out so that only a couple of inches darted in and out of my pussy, finding my G Spot with every inward thrust.

"Ohhhh! *Yesssss!*" I shouted.

"Oh...I'm so hot," he moaned. "I haven't been with a woman in awhile, and your pussy is sooo hot!"

I worried for a second that things would come to a quick end, but he gathered himself and proceeded to fuck me all...night...long!! I couldn't believe it!

"You have such great control, Rick!" I told him at one point. "I've never been with a man who could keep it up...so...long!"

The animal in me had taken over, and I didn't even mind when I realized I had left the shades up and the light on, making it more than likely that someone in the neighborhood was watching us! (There was an old lady, for instance, across the way who'd often complained about my walking around my bedroom naked with the shades open; but I paid her no mind. If she didn't want to see what was going on in my bedroom, why did she look?! To be honest, though, I guess there was a bit of an exhibitionist in me. It seemed so much more exciting, knowing someone might be watching!)

Rick was as ravenous as I was for lovemaking, and so, over and over, he brought me from one shattering climax to another. No other man had ever been able to satisfy my almost insatiable urges before! He was cocking the hell out of me!

I grew a bit dizzy toward the end, his nonstop hard-on practically splitting me in two. Amazingly enough, his organ seemed to grow larger and larger with each thrust; he was filling my cunt as it had never been filled.

I finally reached a point I had never reached before with a man, feeling for the first time in my life that I had reached my limit.

"Come for me, baby," I pleaded, reaching back to cup his huge balls in one hand and tickle his bottom with my other hand, hoping the extra stimulation would make him lose control.

"Come for me baby!" I kept saying, madly gyrating my hips to ream him good.

Any other man would have come under my influence. But he wouldn't stop!

Raising my feet over my head with one hand and furiously ravaging my clit with his other, he fiercely rammed his iron-hard weapon into my twink over

and over and over until I was so overcome I
actually *passed out!*

Later that morning, when I awoke to find his
arms wrapped around me and his beautiful bare
body lying next to mine (his cock still sticking up in
the air), I showered him with kisses, and I *knew...*

I *knew* I wanted to stay with him for the rest of
my life.

G.G.'s Story: Read Me A Bedtime Story

If you're asking me what one of my best love-making memories is, it would be a direct result of my being asked to contribute a story to this book.

I had told my husband that I'd been asked to submit details about a great sex experience, to see what his reaction would be.

Thankfully, he reacted in a very supportive way, encouraging me to write about anything I cared to write about. (Although he seemed a bit worried I might chose to write about one of my experiences with someone else.)

I assured him that, whatever story I chose to write about, it would be about *us* (and that it would be anonymous). But, then again, he is the best lover I've ever had (by far), and so choosing to share one of our experiences was a no-brainer. I also made to sure to get his approval to reveal our most intimate moments.

We both suggested possible ideas, of times we'd especially remembered fondly, but we could not agree on which experience was the best. And then, something happened that made the choice absolutely clear.

Chris came home late one night with a story in hand, a short story he'd written in his office after work, about a time we had made love in his car. I was preparing the tub for a bath when he excitedly handed me the story. When he took notice of the fact that I was already occupied, he thoughtfully offered to read his story to me while I bathed. (That was a very romantic thing to do!)

Chris had one proviso, however: that I had to

masturbate as he read the story. Feeling a blush come over my face, I thought about it for a moment and then agreed, thinking it probably would be fun. (We were newlyweds and were still in the stage where we were eagerly looking for new things to do with each other, sexually. This was one of them; I'd never done myself in front of him.)

Getting in the tub, the water lapping at my thighs as it rose in level, Chris sat down Indian-style on the rug by the tub and began to read his story. The writing wasn't great, but he had succeeded in rekindling memories from our experience having sex in his car, when we were dating. (We'd made love in it, while it was parked in his parents' driveway!)

I pulled the plug in the tub to let the water out again as he read, and he looked at me, puzzled.

"What are you doing?" he asked.

"You'll see!" I said.

On and on his story went, and it did make me feel real sexy all over again. I started to breath heavier, and I could feel the inside of my twat getting moist.

Plugging up the tub's drain again, I then eased myself into a new position: sliding my bottom toward the gushing faucet, I placed my pedicured feet on either side of the faucets against the tile wall, maneuvering my body so that the water stream cascaded *directly onto my slit.*

My husband did a double-take. Pausing for a split second to look at my hips writhing and my fingers holding my pussy lips open wide for the water to do me better, my husband was definitely aroused. He looked over briefly, giving me a sexy smile, as if to say, "you Devil, you!"

I was actually anxious to do this for Chris. This is the way I used to do myself in my bathtub at home in my single days, and I'd told Chris about it, but I never performed my ritual for him before. (I don't know why the idea seemed so exciting, but I felt like I HAD to share this with him.)

I began to groan involuntarily with the effects the torrent of water was having on me, delightfully pounding my pussy (the faucet was turned up all the way). As the tub began to fill, my pussy became immersed in water and so I was having trouble maintaining contact with the flow. Noticing this, my husband, without missing a beat in reading his story, put his huge left hand under my butt and raised my bottom up enough so that the water could continue to do me (he even directed my body to the right spot).

The thought of him watching me perform this

private act really made me want to come. In fact, I began to get those telltale *I'm-about-to-come* tingles within a minute or two!

Sensing I was approaching the point of no return, Chris turned the faucet to make the water a few degrees *hotter* just as he was reading about the part in his story about whipping off my panties and going down on me for the first time...but I drowned out the rest, because I then absolutely *lost* it.

The water upon my pussy made me feel as if I was being tongued by ten or more lovers at once. Every part of my cunt was being aroused, from my clit down to by labia, inside my hole, even lapping at my bottom.

"Oh GOD!" I screamed, the water splashing over the sides of the tub and onto Chris during the throes of my orgasm. There was the feeling of disbelief as the surge of power overtook me.

"Too fast, I came too fast," I said, panting deeply, still dizzy from my climax.

"No, that was great!" Chris said, reassuringly, as he kissed and hugged me. He didn't seem to mind the fact that he was getting wet in the process.

Sweetly holding my head to his shoulder while caressing my hair, I felt very lucky to be his wife. He was such a wonderful man! (And, because of that, I felt comfortable doing things with him that I'd never done before.)

Getting the look of a boyish prankster on his face, Chris, as if on impulse, dropped the computer printout of his story on the bathroom floor. He then stood up and, with a smile in his eyes, stripped off his clothes and joined me in the tub.

Moving so that my back was to the faucet, I instructed him to lean backward on the opposite side of the tub, and put his feet on the tile wall behind me. Teasing both of his nipples with my fingers (they are as sensitive as mine), I made him moan with pleasure. Then, I moved my hands down to his scrotum and petted his balls until his prick started to inflate.

"I just love watching you grow!" I told him.

His fabulous cock grew bigger and bigger as I massaged the skin between his balls with one hand, using the other to softly hold and caress his left ball. Seeing his engorged penis head rise above the water made my nipples get hard and my pussy wet again.

After a minute or two, however, he began to lose his hard-on.

"You cold?" he asked.

"Yes, a bit," I said.

And, with that, he took my hands and raised me

up out of the water, escorting me from the tub like the true gentleman he is. He then dried me off from head to toe, with a warm, fluffy towel.

I couldn't get over what a romantic gesture that was! And, I might add, his pampering only made me want him inside me that much more.

Anyway, this story would not be worth writing if it ended there. What happened *afterward* is actually what made the night so special.

Cuddling in bed, Chris lowered his head to suck my left nipple (which he discovered awhile ago is my most sensitive nipple). Meanwhile, his left hand was stroking the bottom of my thighs, which produced tingling sensations in my pussy, and a strong desire to have sex.

He kept this up -- sucking my nipples and caressing my thighs -- until I was *red* hot, to the point where I could hardly hold still. My breathing growing heavy and my moans louder, he then took his right hand (while tongue lashing my nipple) and parted my vulva to expose my clit to his left hand's middle finger. Placing that finger on top of my clit (after quickly inserting it in my cunt for some lubricating nectar), he ever so softly rubbed back and forth, back and forth, repeatedly in that fashion, never showing any sign of increasing his pace or pressure.

The regular rhythm was maddeningly pleasurable...His fingers felt so soft, but the effect was so...potent!

Gripping both sides of the bed now, I was surprised to find his little ruse getting to me so quickly, my body tensing, my climax about to come on.

Then, *oh God, oh God*...bang! It *hit* me like a ton of bricks! Screaming *oh!*...my body was rolling all over the bed, convulsing, trembling, coming like mad! Throwing his body over mine and holding me in place, Chris comforted me as I struggled to breathe.

"That was nice," he said in soothing tones, which I referred to as "The Voice."

(That's one of the little jokes we share. I noticed early on in our relationship, that when Chris feels sexy or he meets a woman he finds attractive, he unconsciously speaks in deep, thick, breathy and sexy tones. I often scold him playfully not to use that voice with any other woman -- because I know its seductive effect on women. He wasn't aware of his use of "The Voice" nor the fact that it absolutely drove women *wild* for him, until I pointed it out to him.)

Anyway, even as I cuddled with Chris, calming down after my orgasm, he lit my fires again.

Taking the index and middle fingers of his left hand, he began petting my labia, alternating that stroking action with quick, shallow penetrations into my vagina.

Then, he did something he'd never done to me before. Now working my left nipple over with his hot tongue, he pushed his fingers up my vagina until they were directly over my G Spot. Simultaneously putting his thumb (which had been deftly dipped in my wetness) over my clit, he massaged both my G Spot and my clitoris *at the same time.* In no time, I was delirious from the electrifying effect the double-attack had inside my brain and my body.

"Oh, oh, ohhhhhhhh!" I cried. "Oh God!!!!!!!!"

Bam! That orgasm was so strong I didn't know what hit me!

As I was rocking and rolling on the sheets, Chris kept up his assault on my senses until I had to beg him to stop.

"No, no!" I pleaded, pulling his still-moving fingers out of my cunt.

I thought he'd be the death of me!

Still sucking my left tit hard, his tongue massaging my lower breast, much of which was in his mouth, I felt Chris maneuvering his enflamed cock against my slit, rubbing it tantalizingly up and down the length of my vulva. Then, I felt him guide his stiff member slowly into my cunt.

"Oh...*God!*" I exclaimed.

I was on fire again, before I'd had time to fully recover from my last orgasm. Suddenly feeling a desperate need for his cock, I took Chris' cute bottom in both of my hands and made him plunge his hard-on deeply inside of me. That was my way of letting him know I was ready to be fucked good and hard.

And that's when Chris pulled another surprise on me. Once he got me going with a few minutes of moderately paced deep thrusting, he again titillated my clitoris with his thumb, and then (how he did this, I don't know), he stuck his middle finger back into my cunt (his cock still inside me, fucking away), using it directly on my G Spot, like a throbbing penis, bouncing the shit out of my G Spot while his cock's insistent penetrations tickled me deeply inside.

I could not imagine at the time what he was doing to me (I didn't feel his finger slip in above his busy cock, and so I didn't realize it was there), but it absolutely blew my mind!

I had his mouth squeezing the shit out of my nipple, his humongous prick fucking the shit out of my cunt, his thumb teasing the hell out of my clit, and now his middle finger massaging my G Spot and...well, as you can imagine, I couldn't take much of that multi-pronged attack, if you will.

"Chris...Chris!" I panted. "No!...Ba-*by!!!!*"

Bam! He sent me over the top again, this orgasm blowing up inside me like you wouldn't believe. My eyes were rolling...I was in disbelief, as the extreme *power* of it floored me, overtaking my ability to function, or even think.

Breathing hard from overexcitement, I begged Chris to stop fingering me, telling him I couldn't take anymore. I was shaking like a leaf. I put my hand to my forehead, trying to steady my reeling mind.

"What was THAT?" I asked, not knowing quite what he had done to make me come so hard. "Did you use your *finger* inside of me while your *cock* was inside of me?"

"Wouldn't you like to know?" he teased, using "The Voice." (He later told me what he'd done, so I could pass that along to you.)

He was kissing my neck, and I could feel myself instantly getting aroused again. Marvelling at Chris' mastery of my body, I realized at that moment that part of the excitement of being with him is my awareness that he knows exactly how to play my body to make me as hot as he likes, whenever he likes...and that he possesses the power to make me want him, again and again.

Well, he made me want him again.

Lying on his right side (with me on my back), he began to slip-slide his cock inside me again. Using his left knee to thrust his hard-on into my cunt with strong, quick insertions, he was waking up every nerve in my body. My nipples were achingly taut, my hot juices were coming down in a flood...

This went on for ten or more minutes, every thrust devastating my senses.

"Oh no!" I whispered breathlessly, realizing how very hot his insertions had made me already. "You're going to make me come again!"

"Yes, yes," he intoned. "I'm going to make you come again!" he intoned.

"You're going to break me in two!" I said incredulously.

And then, with his right hand holding my pussy lips open, exposing my rock hard clit, making it all that more vulnerable to him, he went *wild* on my upper vulva with his left hand. I mean...wild! He was furiously rubbing my clitoris up and down, up and down, in a way no man has ever done before. I mean, no woman could withstand this very long, without coming.

At this point, I knew he had me -- my climax was

inevitable.

And then...WHAM! And, when I came, I thought I was going to *die!*

Seconds beforehand, I was actually *scared.* I KNEW the orgasm was going to be HUGE, and I really thought I was going to pass out -- and I nearly *did.*

"Oh, oh, I'm so *dizzy,* I'm so dizzy!" I said, barely able to breathe.

My heart was pounding like mad -- boom! boom! boom! -- and my body was bouncing uncontrollably from the aftershocks of my climax.

"It's OK, it's OK," Chris reassured me, in very soothing tones.

The inside of my cunt was undulating madly -- boom! boom! boom! -- and my vulva was spasming like crazy, which had never ever happened to me before. It felt as if my pussy was going to leave my body and fly off on its own! Meanwhile, my body was shaking all over at the same time!

"Don't worry -- just relax!" he whispered.

"What was THAT?" I said, absolutely blown apart from one of the biggest orgasms I'd ever experienced.

"That was the Big One, hon," he joked.

But it was!!!

"Oh, I'm so dizzy!" I said again. "Please, I can't take anymore," I pleaded, crying a bit because of over-stimulation and joy.

"No more tonight," he quickly replied reassuringly, lovingly pulling the blankets over me, tucking me in. I picked up the concern in his voice. "No more tonight, hon. Don't worry. Just relax."

I attempted to get up, so I could give him some attention (he hadn't come all night), but, as I told him, "I can barely move!"

(It's a strange feeling when you're kind of paralyzed by the effects of an immense orgasm, and you can't hardly move.)

"Don't move, hon," he cooed, pushing my body back down on the bed when he saw me struggling to get up off the mattress. "Relax, and enjoy the feeling."

Kissing me on the neck, he sent me off into the deepest sleep of my life with the words: "Night, night, hun."

I want to tell you: NO ONE had EVER done me like THAT before!

The next morning I woke him, telling him how great he'd been the night before, and how well I'd slept as a result.

"I've never slept so well!" I admitted.

I snuck one hand down to caress his balls and

reawakened his member, when he suddenly got up, saying he had to go to the john. As he walked there, I watched him admiringly.

"You look like one of those statues with the great big penises pointing up!" I said. He did!

Returning to bed after washing his cock off (he was always considerate in that way, scrupulous in attending to his hygiene), I grabbed the bottle of olive oil I kept by the bed for massages, and anointed the shaft of his cock with lubricant.

I began jerking him off with my left hand (my thumb strategically placed so as to rub his sensitive frenulum below the head of his cock at the top of my upstroke), while caressing his balls with my right hand. I pulled on his cock until it was thick and swollen, like a tight, clenched muscle.

His cock head started to drip, and his body was wriggling uncontrollably, and so I knew I was giving him a damn good hand job.

"Come for me, baby," I cooed in his ear. "Come for me! And then I'll lick it all up!"

"Oh," he sighed, letting me know my words had softened him up, so to speak.

"Come for me, baby," I repeated, my words speeding up with the increased speed of my hand job. "I love watching you come all over yourself!"

Although his hard-on grew larger and larger (the

head became so swollen that it was *shiny*), I couldn't bring him off...that is, until I remembered what really got to him.

I started to kiss his lips, all the while working his cock over in a way that would have made a lesser man come a long time ago. That brought him to a bouncing, ear-piercing climax.

He was shooting all over the place! He must have shot a gallon of cum, the underside of his cock just throbbing and throbbing with each spurt.

I was enjoying seeing what I'd done to him. I just *love* watching him come!

Moving my head down to his cute, flat, sexy belly, I found myself doing what I'd never wanted to do with any other man before, *eagerly licking up all of his cum!*

It was a real turn-on, to me as well as to him. I caught his shocked expression as he raised his head up, to look down at me. He then laid his head back down with a groan.

"Oh, *man!*" he said.

"Just think," I told him in a sexy voice, as I brought my head up to his. "Last night and all of this would never have happened had you not read me your sexy story!"

Speaking of which, I think that shows you the value of a great bedtime story!

R.B.'s Story: Reach Out & Touch Him

My job requires me to do a good amount of traveling, which can be kinda rough on my relationship with my husband. Some day soon I am definitely going to have to get off the road, even if I have to find another job.

But, in the meantime, I've discovered a novel and exciting way to keep the home fires burning hot when I'm away.

It's a way that might seem a bit bold to you at first. But, trust me, if you try it, I guarantee you'll like it!

I got the idea from zoning out to the TV tube late one night alone in a hotel room. Suddenly, one of those suggestive commercials came on, for a phone sex service, and I thought...hmmm... if it works between strangers, why not between husbands and wives?

So, I immediately phoned my husband. It was just after 11 o'clock where I was (in California), and so it was already past 2 a.m. where my husband was (in Boston); but the idea had gotten me so worked up I just *had* to call him! Plus, I figured he wouldn't mind my awakening him in the middle of the night for the kind of fun I had in mind.

My husband's voice sounded groggy and concerned when he answered the phone, clearly expecting bad news.

"Hi, honey," I purred.

"Sweetheart...what's up?" he said solicitously.

"Nothing, baby, I just miss you," I replied, the tone of my voice calming him down instantly.

James is a very patient and understanding man,

and so he showed no sign of being upset with me for calling so late.

"I just wanted to hear your voice," I continued. "I miss you sooooo much!"

"Mmmm," he responded in his bedroom voice. "Me too!"

"Plus...I have an unusual *idea*," I offered. "And I thought you'd *really* like it."

"Really?" he answered, the curiosity apparent in his voice. My sexy attitude must have gotten him going.

"Yes," I said teasingly. "I think we ought to have a bit of phone sex."

"Phone sex?" he repeated, in a breathy way.

"Yes...*phone sex*! I'll do myself for you, and then you do yourself for me!"

"Hmmm...I dunno," he said.

"Don't you want to know what I'm wearing?" I teased.

"Well...*Yes*," he said. "What *are* you wearing?"

"I'm wearing that lace teddy you gave me, with the push-up bra and snap-open crotch. It made me feel sexy allll day long," I said in a hot-and-bothered voice. "It made me think of you, which made me very wet and hot. And now, I've got to *do* something about it."

"You do?" he replied, picking up on the game.

"Yes...Right now, I'm releasing my nipples from the tops of my cups, and I'm stroking them... Ohhh! It's getting so *hot* in here!"

"Oh...You're making me hard," he replied.

"Is your poor cock getting hard?" I cooed.

"Yes...I'm going to have to take off my underwear, 'cause you made me outgrow it, and now it *hurts!*' he answered.

"It must be *so* large!" I said.

"Yes," he said (and I could hear rustling sounds as James removed his briefs).

"I'm sooo wet," I continued. "I think I'm going to have to touch myself!"

Moving my fingers over my crotch, I began rubbing my slit up and down through my lingerie.

"Oh, James...my cunt is *so* wet for you!"

"Ohhh," he said, sounding as if I was really turning him on.

"You're not touching yourself yet, are you?" I whispered, playfully scolding him.

"Yes, yes; I'm rubbing my cock up and down," he replied.

"No you don't!" I said, pretending to be stern with him. "You wait until I'm through, and then I'm going to *tell* you what I want you to do for me."

I'd never ordered James about in this way before, but he didn't complain. (And it was too fun!)

"OK," he said reluctantly. "So, what are you doing now?"

He was clearly anxious to get a mental picture of what was going on in my room.

"I'm taking out the vibrator you gave me, and I'm undoing the snaps at the bottom of my teddy," I said, my voice dripping with sex.

"You took the vibrator with you?" he asked, clearly surprised, but not at all upset.

"Yes, James. And I've turned it on," I said, putting the vibrator up to the mouthpiece, so he could hear it humming. "And now I going to rub it up and down my vulva, which is *slippery* wet."

"Ohhh," he sighed involuntarily. "You're getting me so *aroused!*"

"That's OK," I said, "so long as you don't *do* anything about it until I say so!"

"I'll try," he replied. "What are you doing *now?*"

"Ohhh...I'm easing the vibrator into my cunt. Ohhh! One inch...two inches...three...Uh, and I'm fingering my clit with my other hand...Oh!...My clitoris is so hard, like a little pearl!"

"Damn," he said. "I can't stand being here where I can't see what you're doing!"

"Are you getting frustrated, honey?" I continued. "It would be *great* if you were here...If you were here, you'd see that I'm now rubbing my clit, with my middle finger..." I sucked air through my lips, in reaction to the deep, internal vibrations my clit was sending through me, in response to my touch.

I was beginning to lose control, my breathing growing heavier. The thought of masturbating in this way, with my husband listening, was *really* turning me on! I was getting off on taking the roles of both an exhibitionist and a big cock teaser.

"I'm raising the speed of the vibrator now," I continued, although it was getting hard to speak. It was fabulous knowing that James was getting more excited with every word I spoke.

"I can hear the vibrator," my husband said. "It must be driving you *crazy!*"

"Yes," I said.

Looking down, I could see that the red rubber phallus rhythmically penetrating me with my quickening wrist motions was *glistening* wet now with my juices. I described the scene, in detail, to James.

"I absolutely *dripping* wet," I told him.

"I'm dripping wet, too," he said.

"You are?" I said, knowing exactly what he meant. When James gets excited, sticky, clear drops of seminal fluid slowly pour out of his swollen pink cock head.

Thinking of James' cock dripping in that way gave me a devilishly sexy idea all of a sudden, which I imagined would blow his mind. Talking like a dominatrix, I said:

"Well, you know that pre-cum that's coming out of your prick? I want you to take one of those drops off your hard-on with one of your fingers and then *taste* it!... Are you doing that?"

"What?" he asked, obviously shy about doing what I'd told him to do.

"You heard me!" I said, struggling to talk as my finger fucking was growing more furious. "Just *do* it!...Now, what does it *taste* like?"

"Oh, baby, you're getting me so hot," he moaned. "You're making me want to come!"

"Not until *I* come," I replied. "Now, what did it taste like?" I repeated. "I bet it tasted nice."

"It's kinda salty," he said.

"Yes, and I bet you liked that." I said, playing the vamp. "See what I make you do?"

"Yes, baby," he answered, playing the role of the

submissive sex slave. "I'll do whatever you say."

"Yes, you *will*," I said, my finger action sending me into a frenzy. James had never been subservient before during sex, and it was a revelation to me at how *hot* that was!

"And...what are you doing *now?*" he asked.

"Now...I'm rubbing my clit even harder, and fucking myself...even faster...with...with the vibrator...I'm going...I'm going to *come* for you!" (I was already most of the way there!)

"Yes, yes, *come* for me!" he panted.

The sound of his deep voice pushed me that much faster toward my climax, and I was no longer able to continue my running commentary.

I could feel my face convulse as the tension in my cunt was building and building...and then I felt the growing sensations from my clit merging with the tickling feelings from the vibrator, the buildup growing larger, and larger...until I closed my eyes shut tight, a burst of colored stars filling my brain with the onset of my climax, my hips grinding away, my busy finger triggering more sensations from my clit.

The fact that I could not scream, for fear that others in the hotel rooms next to me might hear me, only drove me crazier, the need to hold down the volume only making the pressure inside my body that much greater.

"Oh! Oh! Ahhhhhhhhhhhh!" I said, now holding a pillow over my mouth to muffle my screams.

"Yes, yes!" he said.

Removing the pillow, I whispered what I wanted to cry out loud: "Ahhhhhhhhhhhhhhhhhh! Oh! Uh! Ohhh!!"

The phone was silent as I raised my head toward the ceiling, my eyes rolling in disbelief at how good that orgasm had felt.

"Oh baby, baby!" I whispered to James as I switched the vibrator off, a hiss of air escaping from my lips as I deflated like a popped balloon from my high. Panting now, still reeling from my orgasm but finally able to talk again, I told James: "Oh, baby! See what thinking of *you* makes me do? I miss you *so* much!"

Slowly removing the vibrator from my throbbing vagina, I moaned as it re-excited me on its way out. I was stunned into silence for a few seconds as the last of the waves of pleasure swept over me.

Finally, I told James: "And now I want *you* to do something for *me!*"

"What's that?" he asked, his tone expectant.

"I want you to grab that big cock of yours through that nice soft blanket I bought the other day, and surround it with your fingers so it feels as if your cock is inside my pussy...

"Are you doing it?" I asked, in an imperious tone.

"Yes," he answered softly.

"Good," I replied. "How does that make you feel?"

"It feels great," he sighed. "It makes me feel like coming."

"Not yet!" I said. "Only when I tell you to!"

"Yes, baby," he sighed, my dominatrix act definitely getting to him. "Now, move your hips as if you're fucking me," I ordered. "Are you fucking the blanket, like a good boy?"

"Yes!"

"Good! Now, with your right hand, take your middle finger and run rings around your left nipple, like I would do if I were there!"

"Ohhhh..." he sighed.

"You like it, don't you?" I teased.

"Yes..."

"Pretend I'm the one touching you!"

"Yes," he replied obediently. "Oh...*baby*..."

My husband's moans were beginning to get louder, and so I knew he was following my instructions. (Meantime, imagining him lying there doing himself was *really* making me wet!)

"Good. I like it when you follow my orders," I told him, relishing the dominant role I'd adopted. (I made a mental note to explore that side of me more in future love-making sessions. It was *hot!*)

"OK," I continued, "now do it *faster!*" He didn't answer, but I could hear him breathing heavily. "Does my baby want to come?"

"Yes, yes, I need to come! You've made me sooo hot!"

"No, not yet!" I interjected. "I won't let you come unless you beg me to let you!"

"Please let me come, please let me come!" he whispered, breathing heavier than before.

"Your cock must be *huge!*" I said, sensuously torturing him.

"Yes!" he sighed. "I can't take much more!"

"OK...Now, take your hand off your prick, remove the blanket and *look* at how *big* I've made you!...Are you looking at your cock?"

"Yes," he responded.

"Don't *touch* it! Just look at it!"

"Yes, baby," he said breathily.

"What does it look like?"

"It's as hard as a rock, and it's really red!"

"OK," I continued, a really kinky thought popping into my head. "Now, take the middle finger of your right hand and put it in your mouth; make it real wet!...Are you doing that?"

"Yes, baby."

"OK, now run that finger up and down your crack, just like I do...Are you doing that?"

"Mmm..." he moaned.

"It feels nice, doesn't it? I know you like that," I said. "And now, while you're fingering your crack, take your left hand and jerk yourself off...just like you do when I'm away and you get hard, thinking of my naked body! Are you thinking of my bare breasts?"

"Oh!...Yes!..."

"Jerk it *faster*...and *harder! Come* for me, baby!" I commanded him. "You want to come, don't you, baby?"

"Yes!...Yes!" he said. "I'm...I'm...*going to come for you, baby*...I'm...Ohhh!"

My husband was now yelling as his climax tore into him. I had to move the earpiece away, his cries were so piercing.

"Sounds like you enjoyed yourself, sweetheart," I teased, once his yells had subsided. "Did you shoot all over yourself?"

"Yes," he whispered almost inaudibly.

"Good! Now, sweet dreams!" I said, hanging up on him.

I stopped for a moment, smiling to myself, enjoying the mental picture I had. I envisioned my husband panting, naked, his cock still semi-hard, his belly covered in cum.

I was really excited about what we'd just done! *We were definitely going to have to do that again,* I thought.

And then my fingers, as if on automatic, started teasing my cunt again, using my wetness to lubricate my labia and then my stone-hard clit. (Listening to my husband jerk off at my command had made me so *hot!*)

Taking the index and middle fingers of my left hand, I began to fuck my cunt, imagining that it was James' cock inside me. Over and over, faster and faster, I massaged my G Spot with the tips of those fingers, my pussy growing hotter and wetter and wider, my G Spot swelling up to the size of a small egg as I made swift circles around it.

Simultaneously stimulating my clit with my right hand, I furiously frigged and fucked myself into oblivion.

Passing out a few seconds later, I slept more

sweetly that night than I've ever slept, all alone in a hotel, far from my husband.

Two days later, when I returned home, my husband told me how hot that experience had been for him. And that he wanted to do it again.

So, ever since, we've incorporated phone sex into our marriage, which has decidedly taken a turn for the better! (Plus, it's kind of fun to have our own little naughty secret!)

Although it's no substitute for the real thing, our liaisons by phone have enabled James and myself to share some very beautiful, intimate moments together when I'm far away somewhere, on the road.

L.C.'s Story: Rock Steady

The weekend had just come to an end, and I was dreading returning to work as I awoke one Monday morning.

I'd just spent the whole weekend with my new lover Mike and I wasn't ready to put my nose to the grindstone again.

Fortunately, because I own my own business, I felt I could afford a little more playtime before dragging myself away from my lover's body.

I decided to arouse the

dead. Mike was still sleeping, but I couldn't wait anymore. So, I started rolling his right nipple with my thumb and index finger, while sucking his left.

His moaning was exactly what I had wanted to hear. (It meant he was open to having some fun.)

Mike's sexy reactions to my playing with his body always turned me on, and so it wasn't long before I felt my juices dripping down from within.

Abandoning his right nipple, I let my hand wander down to his belly to see if my teasing had had its desired effect. I was glad to discover that it had. His passion was rampant, so to speak.

Running my fingers up and down his shaft made Mike squirm in the sheets. Watching his legs spasm and his back arch raised my own temperature. My nipples were poking straight up.

"I see I've gotten your attention," I whispered in his ear. He could not seem to speak, apparently overwhelmed by what I was doing to him, but he let out a moan in response.

"I'm not going to see you until next weekend," I continued, "so I need a big send-off...*now.*"

As I teased his balls by gently rubbing them up and down, his groans grew more excited.

"What would you like me to do to you?" he finally managed to ask, in a whisper, weakened by the onslaught of my caresses.

"Whatever you'd like," I said, smiling broadly.

I could tell by the look in his eyes that he'd already thought of something special. He was always coming up with something new; that's one thing that makes being with him so exciting.

He'd taught me more positions than I'd ever known, and more about my body than I'd ever known; but, it was the passion and intensity of what he had done to me sexually that made me want him so badly when he was away. And the way he instinctively *knew* what I wanted him to do; the way he always *knew* how to make me come (fast, repeatedly, in so many ways, and from so many locations on my body) made me want him all that much more...But, back to my story:

Mike turned over to lie on his left side and began to suck my right nipple in his own special way, making me hot with the anticipation of his bringing me to a nipple orgasm (he was the only one who had ever made me come solely by sucking my nipples). He was rolling my nipple like a grape with his tongue, while sucking the end of my breast to bring it deeply inside his hot, wet mouth.

If he'd kept that up, I'd inevitably have climaxed, but that wasn't part of his plan this day. While titillating my nipple, he then started stimulating my mound and my inner thighs with his right hand, brushing me lightly, driving me mad.

Too hot and impatient to allow his slow tease to continue, I took matters into my own hands, firmly pushing his hand onto the hot, wet and soft cleft between my legs, to let him know what I needed.

"Ohhh," he murmured upon feeling my wetness, acknowledging my state of arousal.

Initially just tickling my labia, he then massaged each one separately, putting his thumb on one side and his middle finger on the other, gently squeezing them as he slid up and down their slippery surfaces. I'd never felt so good from that part of my body, and I don't think a minute passed before I heard myself groaning, and then screaming, as I realized I was about to have my first *labial* orgasm!

"What are you doing to me?" I asked rhetorically, as the tickling feeling inside me grew, becoming like a knotted ball, that again grew before exploding like a thousand fireworks going off, all over my body (and especially in my head).

"Ummm!" he purred, egging me on in my orgasm. "Yes, let it go, let it go, honey, let it go!"

"Ohhhh!" I screamed, my back arching as waves of ecstacy pounded my body. *"OH!"*

My first labial orgasm ever felt *great*, and deliciously *different* from any other type of orgasm I'd ever experienced -- I can't quite describe it.

Mike continued to lovingly pet my labia for a minute or so after I came, before digging deeper inside my folds, when he felt I was ready for more. Using his index and middle fingers, he began exploring the swollen, egg-sized organ at the top of my vaginal canal -- my G Spot.

First running circles around its circumference, using my juices as a lubricant, he then started to wiggle his fingers in the most unusual way, pressing up into my G Spot (softly) with each up stroke, moving faster and faster, until I felt my toes curling involuntarily, and the muscles in my legs and tummy tensing up...I could not believe it, but he going to make me come again, from my G Spot.

"Ohhhhh, ahhhhhhh!!" I screamed, as a bath of hot fluid filled my cunt, my orgasm breaking over me like someone had broken a huge, magical egg on my head, filled with hot, sexy jism.

Pleasantly shaken, I trembled for what seemed like minutes after the first rush of my orgasm had flashed through the length of my body.

Mike was sweetly hugging me, wrapping his left arm around me, squeezing his nicely sweaty body against mine, rocking me gently and reassuringly, as his fingers continued to rub my G Spot, although much more slowly than before.

Kissing me repeatedly on the neck, Mike rearranged himself until I felt the soft head of his penis touching my pussy lips, which gave me a clue as to what was coming next (no pun intended). I was already quite wasted from the combined effects of numerous orgasms, but I also needed to feel his hardness inside of me.

Still lying on his side, Mike grabbed his swollen penis with his right hand, rubbing its velvety head up and down my pussy until I thought I was going to come again. But, before that happened, he slowly, gently inserted his cock into the outside recesses of my vagina, leaving it there motionless.

Then, pushing on the skin around my clitoris with two fingers on either side of it, he manipulated the hood of my clit so that my clit was alternately exposed and then hooded again, repeatedly.

This became too much for me. Breathing heavily and moaning louder and louder, I think he got the message.

Taking his middle finger, he tantalized me with back and forth movements of increasing speed, reminding me of how he sometimes stroked the strings of his guitar. Like an instrument, he played my clit with increasing intensity and just before I found myself coming again, he simultaneously slipped the full length of his long penis deeply inside of me, increasing the intensity of my orgasm.

"Oh God, oh God, oh God!!" I shouted, as energy bounced every which way in my body.

"Ummm! I can feel your juices dripping down my balls," he cooed into my ear, as my body was being wracked by my climax.

I thought he was just about done with me, but, actually, a whole new scenario was about to unfold. As I laid on my back, my eyes closed, still luxuriating in my last ride to heaven, I felt Mike lift my left leg gracefully and move my legs together in between his, his knees straddling my hips.

On top of me now, Mike proceeded to give me the ride of my life. Rocking me steady, over and over, with an in-and-out moderately-paced rhythm, positioning his penis so that it was stroking me in places and at angles from which he knew he could make me come, he'd keep up his steady rocking until it drove me wild and made me come all over him.

After I'd come, he'd hold me for a short while, and then he'd move his cock further in or further out and rock me from that angle and depth until I came again and again and again.

For a while, he'd balance his body over mine with the lightness of a ballet dancer, his thighs rubbing softly against mine, his toes like springs propelling him back and forth over me, the head of his cock going inside me just a few inches and then out the same amount, over and over, teasing the hell out of my G Spot until I rewarded his pendulum-like efforts with a massive meltdown.

Then, he'd move his knees astride me and slide his hard-on up and in until it was in all the way, and, wiggling his bottom, he'd move it just a couple of inches in each direction, with a passionate, rock-steady rhythm, until I came yet again.

All the while, he was talking to me, his voice and words making me want to come again.

"I've got you just where I want you," I remember him whispering, his hands holding my hands down above my head, his legs surrounding mine, his body delightfully pinning me down. Oh man, I could feel my body melt after he said that.

I swear I'm pretty sure I came at least 10 more times once he started rocking me steady, but I can't say for certain. I can tell you that, toward the end, I thought I was going to pass out.

"Come for me," I said to him more than once, hoping he'd let me off the hook so to speak, but he'd just respond that he wasn't ready to quit yet, and that he was going to make me come again, which he *did*, again and again. He completely rocked me into oblivion.

I was beginning to get overexcited now, so I finally said, in a voice weakened to a whisper by too much pleasure, "no more, no more!"

Understanding that he'd pushed me to the limit, he gave in to my words of surrender, but not without a bit more teasing.

"Oh, so you're throwing in the towel!" he said playfully. "Well, you'll have to *beg* me to stop."

"Please stop," I said, but not as convincingly as I would have liked. Only a woman who's *really* been fucked knows how hard it is to summon up the strength to say anything, let alone convince a strong, nonstop lover to stop.

"Beg me to stop," he repeated.

"Please, I beg you to stop," I said, laughing as only a woman who's been done to completion would understand. Mike had gotten me to say what no other man had *ever* gotten me to say (that is, to *stop*), from experiencing too *much* pleasure at his hands.

"And come for me," I said once again.

"OK, baby," he said, in a loving tone. "I'm going to come for you."

And he did. But not before pushing me over the edge one more time, with his final, lung-deep furious thrusting, which nearly shook the bed off its posts and seemed to go on for minutes.

I squeezed my vaginal muscles after his spasms and screams of pleasure had subsided, hugging his still-hard penis in my love canal. He relaxed his body over mine, surrounding me with his arms, covering me with his wonderful, warm, muscular torso like a living, breathing blanket, cuddling with me in a way only true lovers could appreciate, as we both drifted off in a rhapsodic haze.

"Shit!" I said, when I'd finally come back to the surface, realizing all of a sudden that I was long overdue at my place of business. Glancing at the alarm clock, I noticed it was 11 o'clock.

"Eleven o'clock?" I said incredulously. *We'd been making love for more than TWO hours!*

My mother was going to be *furious* with me! She had expected me to arrive by 10, our normal opening time, and I was *way* late!

With the languorous effects of a sound fucking still upon me, it took me another hour to get ready to leave (my body wobbly and my mind, anesthetized). Mike had taught me how wonderfully devastating he could be, just by rocking me steady.

The rest of the day turned out all right...except that I suffered from the incapacitating effects of the morning's lovemaking session, all day long... allllll day long...

D.D.'s Story: Wake Me Up!

It was the night before our second month's anniversary, and Dan took me out to a nice restaurant to celebrate the eve of the event...

It had been (and has been) a dream relationship with Dan -- the kind you crave, but often give up on finding.

My friends had been teasing me for quite some time about it, actually, because I've never had a negative thing to say about Dan. Some have even said I've become a different person since meeting him, but I think that's exactly the way it's supposed to be. Or perhaps, I'm the same person, only

better…happiness will do that!

Anyway, when we returned home that night Dan looked awfully tired, and so I encouraged him to go to bed and get some rest. I read a bit, enjoying the feeling of lying next to the great new man in my life, all 6 feet 3 inches of his beautiful naked body exuding a warmth that made me decide to turn out the light and snuggle with him.

"You're the most beautiful man in the world to me," I whispered in his ear before I laid my head down on my pillow. I don't know if he heard me, but it didn't really matter. Dan has made me feel so content.

Later on (I'm a light sleeper), maybe 2 or 3 in the morning, I felt Dan sidle up and spoon with me from behind, his left hand now cuddling my right breast. I love it when he does that. It makes me feel secure and loved.

I was half-awake, thinking about how much I cared for Dan, and then I decided I had to tell him something. Turning over to whisper in his left ear, I said:

"These have been the happiest two months of my life!"

Dan, groggy, opened his eyes briefly and responded: "My pleasure, baby," kissing my left hand several times.

After we both had adjusted ourselves (I was now on my back, and Dan on his side, both of us buck naked), I felt one of Dan's warm large hands tenderly rest itself on my right hip, occasionally stroking the soft flesh of my upper thigh.

Because Dan had been so tired that night, and also because up until that time we had never made love after we'd fallen asleep, I was sure things would end there.

But Dan's hand began to wander over to my mound, where his fingers began lovingly stroking the sensitive tops and insides of my thighs...so lightly, a feather's touch would have felt heavy in comparison...and then -- I couldn't tell if he was touching me there at first he was so soft and gentle about it -- I began to feel a tickling feeling up and down my vulva.

"Oh!!" I sighed, opening my thighs to him. "I thought you were tired," I added, joking around.

"I just couldn't let you get away with saying something so *nice*, without returning the favor!" he said.

Hmm. I made a mental note that Dan really, really appreciated my sincerely loving remarks. That was very valuable information. I thought: *I*

*could use that to help ignite other nights of passion
in the future.*

Awakening my senses now with sensual kisses
on the side of my neck, Dan spread apart my labia
and pulled up on the V at the top of my slit, to
raise the hood off my clit for better access. He
then started doing a maddeningly slow and soft
butterfly's fluttering above my clitoris with his
fingers.

Suddenly, I realized how very hot I was! Being
awakened by a sexual advance was so shocking
on some level that I was already feeling like I
might come at any moment!

I was soooo hot from his barely perceptible
fingerwork and the excitement of being taken
unexpectedly that, indeed, I CAME within a few
minutes!

"Oh, Dan, oh!"

I was almost embarrassed by how quickly I had
come. But, that orgasm was...incredible! No man
had ever sensitized me to the extent that I could
come so easily, with so little pressure!

My eyes were rolling in my head with pleasure
as I felt Dan's hand moving lower, separating my
labia with two fingers as he laid his long and
talented middle finger to rest entirely over the

length of my slit.

Always full of surprises in bed, Dan then did something new and astonishing. He began wiggling his middle fingertip to tease the bottom V of my vagina. I didn't realize how responsive that part of me was until he started to play with it (nobody before Paul had ever stimulated that part -- whatever it's called -- and I hadn't discovered it myself, either, in my years of self-exploration).

Wriggling uncontrollably now, I was amazed at what he was doing to me as he manipulated it. I was shocked when I realized that Dan could tickle it in such a way that this wonderful, previously unknown source of pleasure was likely to make me come again.

Two or three minutes went by and Dan just kept using my growing wetness to lubricate and work the tiny piece of flesh over and over until...*oh my God!*...I could feel my next climax emanating and building right from that spot...*OHHHH!*...my body was soon writhing in ecstacy, bouncing all over the bed...Dan's fingers flicking that special spot faster and faster as I came until I had to peel his fingers off of me...*Oh!*...it was too much! I needed to catch my breath!

Finally, when I was settling back to Earth from

that high, I realized I was now thoroughly dripping wet (as evidenced by the wet spot I'd made on the bed, under my bottom).

Dan's long and wonderfully *knowing* fingers continued to work their magic. His ring finger was resting over the crack of my bottom while his middle finger was inside my pussy, pressed firmly up against my swollen G Spot, while his *thumb* was tantalizing my upper vulva! In this three-fingered way, he began a more intense assault on my senses, this time shaking those areas with strong, masculine back and forth motions that affected my entire middle -- he'd launched a three-front assault on my bottom, my cunt and my clit!

"Dan!...Dan, what are you doing to me?" I panted, stroking his head urgently, as it became clear how potent his massage would be.

Little balls of delight were growing in each of the three areas he was stimulating...until...*BABY!*...he got me again, an orgasm going off in my head like an explosion of light and sound and pulsations...my body shaking so violently that Dan hugged me and soothed, "It's OK, baby, just relax, it's OK, baby."

I could *not* believe it...my soul was off somewhere, way above me, shot clear around the world.

"You make me come so *easily*," I panted as I regained a little sense of composure.

Yet, with a little rest, I was craving Dan's cock inside me.

Reaching over to touch him, Dan, lying on his right side, immediately understood what I wanted. Smoothly as could be, he raised my thighs above his legs and directed his hugely enflamed cock sideways, so that its soft head massaged my clit awhile before he slipped some of its impressive length ever so slowly into the outer recess of my cunt.

My body was suddenly on fire! I needed him badly, I wanted him to just...take me!

But he's a big teaser and loves to get me really, really hot before he really goes wild, and so he just rested his big cock within the outer few inches of my cunt, softly cooing to me, *"oh, is my baby getting hot?,"* as both of his hands lightly caressed the highly sensitive skin on my breasts, my tummy, my hips, and my thighs -- ALL over!

The heat and size of his idle cock was burning my insides, driving me crazy. So I felt the need to wiggle my hips or go absolutely mad!

Dan knows how to make me desperate for his cock...and although I knew what he was doing...the game he was playing was working!

"Ummm," he purred. "It feels like someone melted butter inside of you! You're sooo hot, too!"

Dan's words were like spraying gasoline on top of a fire. By now, I was wriggling wildly, trying to get more of Dan's cock, but he held me at bay... Until...FINALLY he gave me some promise of relief from the flames that were burning me up.

He began to move his cock! The movement coming after such a long period of teasing made its effect that much more startling. My G Spot was balling up, definitely about to send me over the top, with the first few exciting parrying motions of Dan's stiff member. (He's the first man I've been with who knows how to *do* my G Spot with his cock.)

"Let's get your G Spot going, baby," he cooed in my ear, sending shivers up and down my body.

"How do you know so much about my body?" I purred, but he only said "Mmm!" in that sexy baritone of his in response.

Stretching my cunt now with ever more deep penetrations, Dan reached his right arm around my shoulders and began to rock my body as if I was in a cradle, setting up a steady in and out rhythm of ever more cock inches that caused something inside me to build...and...build...and build until I felt I'd literally *explode* from my climax.

"Ohhhhhhh! Ohhhhhhh! Ohhhhhhh!" I cried, my body trembling. I had trouble catching my breath. I reached out and held one of his hips in place.

"No more right now, no more," I panted.

"Oh, baby, I've just *started*," he teased.

With me lying on my back, he on his right side, his virile left hand firmly holding my left thigh above his legs (while his fingers caressed my tender inner thigh), his balls resting on my right thigh (which was surrounded and held in place by his thighs), he acceded to my wishes and gave me a minute or so of downtime, all the while slowly easing his massive erection in to the max.

"I just love being inside you, honey. That's the only place I ever really want to be -- inside of you, making love to you," he told me sweetly, as he eased his thick hard-on all the way into my sheath.

Feeling his cock stretching my pussy to the limit re-electrified my nerves. Then he slowly, slowly, slowly slid his shaft back out, until I could feel his cock head darting in and out of my slit, soon finding my G Spot and settling into one of Dan's "come grooves."

I call Dan's little dances inside me "come grooves." He knows my body so well, all he has to do is to choose a spot inside me with his cock and he instinctively knows how to work it over, with the right depth, the right rhythm, and, man, I'm coming again and again!

(He's a *great* cocksman. He's found all of my "places," even ones I didn't know.)

"Oh...you're going to make me come again!" I gasped, as the head of cock started a warm spot in my G Spot area that grew...and grew...until...

"Ahhhhhh! Ohhhhhh! No more! No more!" I pleaded. "I can't take anymore!"

I was absolutely doubled over with excruciating pleasure, my head bent over my thighs, my feet pulled off the bed, in one big convulsion...I was struggling to breathe...

"I feel sorry for other women," I whispered, still panting, my senses reeling. "They don't know what they're missing!"

Minutes later, Dan's finger got my clit going and I was headed inexorably toward another climax...

"No more! No more!" I begged him after he

made me come yet again, my body quivering all over.

"Oh baby, I know you want some more of my cock!" he teased, in that low growl of his.

This story's not going to sound believable, maybe, but his masterful fingers upon my clit and nipples soon had me begging for *more*.

That's when he went into high gear, furiously but masterfully penetrating me as far as he could go, in kind of a quick corkscrew motion. "Oh, GO on, baby!" I shouted, loving it when he gives it to me hard)...

That went on until my body melted into a pool of cum. I didn't feel like there was anything left of me after that.

Slowly disengaging from me, lying back, he took me in his arms and rocked me gently, as my body kept on shuddering for what seemed like a half hour.

"It's OK, baby, just relax, and go to sleep," he soothed. "Happy anniversary, baby, happy anniversary." (What a nice thing to say and do! He was ready to go to sleep, his cock still ramrod solid, *without having come himself!*)

For a short while, it was all I could do just to catch my breath. I lay there, my chest heaving but otherwise motionless, for about five minutes while Dan stroked my hair.

Once I could move again, I eased my right hand down to cup his balls and asked him: "Do you really want to go to sleep?"

(His cock was *still* sticking up like a pole, as hard as a rock.)

"That's OK, baby, you don't have to do anything. I'm fine," he said.

"You don't want me to touch you?"

"Yes, you can touch me, if you're not too tired," he said sweetly. "I thought you'd be too tired."

"Never," I answered, and I proceeded to give him the best hand job he'd ever gotten.

After making him shoot torrents of hot cum over his athletic torso, I leaned over to coo in his ear:

"And you can wake me up for that anytime!"

J.L.'s Story: Sorority Sisters

What I am about to tell you may shock you. That is, unless you were a sorority sister in college. (Most women who have been in college sororities know that those secret societies are a hotbed of youthful sexual experimentation.) Looking back on those days, I think the college administration *knew* about the intimate escapades that were going on at my sorority, but simply winked at it. After all, it was just a part of growing up.

It was for me, anyway.

I unexpectedly (or, perhaps, *serendipitously*) wound up sharing some tender moments with a sorority sister.

Until now, I've never told this story to anyone.

Cindy was my roommate and close confidant. A stunning blonde from Chicago, Cindy was about 5'10", with long, ravishing legs, delicious, tanned skin, and cute, nicely-shaped medium-sized breasts (with luscious red areolas), whose nipples tantalized the campus -- they were always perky and unfettered behind her loose-fitting T-shirts. It was hard to think of anything else when her tits were pointing up at you like an invitation, through her blouse. (She was well aware of her allure -- she was always finding an excuse, such as tying her shoes, to bend over and seduce you with a quick glimpse of her cleavage.)

We felt a close kinship from the start. She would join me on my bed for nighttime confessions and joking around at the end of a long day of courses and studying. I found it exciting and a bit arousing when she'd put her face close to mine and brush my hair (the warmth of her body and scent of her perfume was intoxicating).

Sometimes, with a little embarrassment, I'd feel myself growing wet when she would tickle me, as she was fond of doing. Sometimes she'd keep it up until I fell on the floor laughing.

My freshman year was a rough one, and so escaping back into the warm confines of my sorority was the one thing I looked forward to all day. Making things worse were my raging hormones, that led to many a night's wet dream or furtive masturbation under the sheets, all the while hoping my roomie wouldn't wake up and notice what I was doing. I would have been mortified if she had!

It wasn't long before rumors spread that girls at my sorority had been seen touching each other in the shower, and that some were even caught kissing each other. I didn't know if the stories were true, but it aroused my curiosity.

Oddly enough, the stories turned me on, and made me fantasize about how it would feel with another girl. I'd only been with one boy by that time, and it hadn't been that great an experience.

The act of losing my virginity was so painful it does not rank high up on my list of my most favorite moments in love-making. The boy who had popped my cherry, Billy, was so inexperienced; he hardly knew what he was doing.

So, I was hungering for a lover who could really send me to the heights I'd fantasized about.

One night, Cindy and I discussed the rumors of

Lesbian activity. Cindy was sure the rumors were true.

"Haven't you ever felt like touching a girl, or kissing one?" she asked me playfully. "Haven't you ever seen breasts so breathtaking you felt you needed to squeeze them, lick their nipples until they were hard, and suck their sweet soft flesh?"

Cindy's words flushed my face with heat, as if my skin was being ignited. Waves of desire over-came me, too, as she lowered her face to mine, her lips inches away from mine. She was seducing me, and I knew it...but I felt powerless to resist.

Before I could think the situation through, her lips were pressing on mine, and I felt a slave to her seduction. Unable and even unwilling to put up a fight now, I let her tongue explore my lips and then penetrate my mouth.

Soon, I was doing the same to her, with the urgency of a teenager hungry for sexual experience. I started to breathe very heavily and I felt as if my blood was boiling. I was, after all, a hot-to-trot teen.

My need for passion overwhelming me, I ex-ploded in a flurry of activity fueled by many years of pent-up desire, desperately wanting to touch, taste, suck, smell and kiss every inch of Cindy's body all at once. My hands were eagerly investigating her body, as hers were mine, as our lips furiously engaged in French kissing. We couldn't get enough of each other.

Cindy quickly took command, however, pushing me on my back and holding my arms down so that she could kiss, pinch, lick and suck my nipples without interference from my frenzied attack on her. I melted away instantly as the tender attack overcame me. I actually thought I would pass out from the overexcitement that comes from experiencing the first taste of great sex that I had craved for so long.

The moment was finally upon me, and I just could not believe it! I could not believe someone was doing this to me! (The fact that it was a girl didn't even matter. Actually, I think it added to the thrill of it.) I was utterly swept away in the emotion of the moment.

Driving me crazy with her passionate attention to my breasts, I screamed and writhed in delightful agony, without thought to whomever might hear me. (Some of the girls later teased me about the noises that came from our room that night, with a wink and a smile).

My nipples were *so* engorged by her devilishly-good sucking! Her expertise made me guess that I was not the first girl with whom she'd done this.

"Oh...oh!" I heard myself groan as Cindy's sexual explorations made me impossibly hot, my pussy aching for attention. It was literally dripping wet now.

Finally, mercifully, I felt one of her hands ease its way down to my crotch, where it rested between my legs, just touching my thin panties.

"Yes, yes," I panted, now desperate for her to do me right then and there.

Without missing a beat, her fingers began running up and down my crack through my panties. *Someone was about to fuck me!* I just could not believe the day had come.

Grabbing the top edges of my panties with both of her hands now, she ripped them off my body. Pushing my legs apart, she then dove into my burning hot pussy, her soft lips and wonderfully hot tongue instantly sending shock waves of pleasure shooting through my body.

"Oh...oh!!!!!!!!!!" I yelled, as she parted my pussy lips and planted her tongue on my clit. Placing my hands on her busy head, I ran my hands through her hair fueled by passion and appreciation.

My body was wriggling wildly now, but Cindy

held my hips down so her tongue could keep up its persistent attack on my senses. And in a moment I knew the thing I had waited for so long was about to happen -- my first great climax was coming on.

It was more powerful than just about any orgasm I've had ever since. I could feel the cum flooding down my vagina -- cum that she eagerly lapped up as she urged me on, saying "yes, yes, good girl, good girl!"

Tears fell down my cheeks as I laughed and cried at the same time, not entirely knowing why the tears came. Kissing my tummy, my breasts and then my face all over, Cindy was very reassuring and patient with me.

"That's a good girl," she kept saying, "it's all right."

Holding me in her arms for what seemed like an eternity, she finally indicated it was her time. Pushing my head with a gentleness but also an authority, in the direction of her pussy, I found myself readily complying with her wishes.

Before I knew it, my cheeks were nestled between her warm thighs, my nose flaring with the unexpectedly delightful scent of her womanhood, my tongue -- as if it had a mind of its own --

obediently reaching out to explore the recesses of her lily-shaped vulva.

"Oh, yessssssss!" she whispered. She seemed more aware of prying ears than I was, always careful to squelch any expressions of ecstacy I made her say.

Taking my head in her hands, Cindy held it firmly to her pussy, not letting me stray a centimeter from her flaming-hot inner surfaces. I was led by passion; everything I did to her came naturally, if not automatically, without any thought.

I absolutely *devoured* her musky pussy with my lips and tongue, delighting in the exotic smell, taste and slippery feel of her most intimate places. I was becoming more and more turned on, too, as I noticed the effect I was having on Cindy.

I was cherishing every moan, groan and wriggle, the arching of her back, the swelling and reddening of her pussy lips, the increased heat and moisture coming from her hole; her every reaction to my touch. It was like a vicarious thrill; I was actually feeling what she was feeling!

Parting her slit with my hands now, I tongued her clitoris wickedly, my hands now madly caressing her legs, from her thighs down to her toes. When I felt her toes curl, I sucked her clit hard and wildly shook my head back and forth, until her body spasmed and her juices came down.

Grasping the sheets tightly in both hands, I could hear Cindy fighting off her natural need to scream, letting loose only with a soft "shhhhhhhhit!"

Her eyes closed now, as if the rapture of the moment was too much, I made my way up Cindy's lovely, bare-naked body to kiss her forehead and rock her in my arms as she went into a deep sleep, which I felt was confirmation that I had been a good lover.

I was proud of what I had done. I just loved feeling the warmth of her smooth, soft skin when I pressed my body close to hers, and the smell of her perfume. In fact, I remember luxuriating in her scent by breathing in one long, slow, deep inhalation after another. I kissed the back of her neck and I, too, fell asleep in a delicious torpor.

It was a very special moment, yet one that would stand out as a very unusual event in my life. Cindy and I only made love to each other a few more times after that (none of those times coming close to the powerful impression left by our first time together).

And then we grew apart, as our interests diverged. I began dating some boys, and she entered into a relationship with another girl, which became serious and lasted for three more years.

But although we were no longer lovers, we remained good friends until graduation day, sometimes meeting for a drink at a local pub.

Years have passed, and now I only occasionally hear from Cindy. (We do exchange Christmas cards, however.)

But, in spite of the fact that I now desire the pleasures that only a man, my husband, can give, I still remember my nights of love-making with Cindy with a great fondness, as if those memories are surrounded by a halo.

Those nights were a necessary part of my growing up and my development. True, too -- they taught me something very valuable about love and tenderness.

C.C.'s Story: Proper Cock Teasing

I have a confession to make. I know cock teasing isn't supposed to be a nice thing, but I just LOVE doing it! Interestingly enough, my boyfriend has never complained about it. In fact, I'm sure he LOVES it!

Actually, I think ALL men secretly love it -- so long as you finish the job, so to speak, at some point.

I mean, who *doesn't* like being teased to the point that you're really, really, hot?!

I truly think cock teasing -- if done *properly* -- should become part of every woman's arsenal of wiles. That way, you always keep your man on his toes, and never allow him to get to where he feels that you're too predictable. You never want him to get bored with your repertoire of sexual ideas.

I guess I should explain myself. I don't mean cock teasing in the traditional sense, where you get the guy real hard and hot to trot by strategically pressing your right thigh on his crotch when French kissing him, or grinding him during a slow dance, only to leave him suffering with blue balls. That's a bit cruel.

What I'm talking about is making my man so hot and bothered for such a long time, that the eventual love-making session that follows my prolonged teasing begins and ends on a much hotter level. I mean, when I'm through cock teasing him, his orgasms are a *lot* stronger. Who wouldn't prefer orgasms that register 7.0 on the Richter scale, to ones that are rather ordinary? I rest my case.

You have to drive your man crazy, though, preferably earlier in the day. Ladies, if you do it properly (in a drawn out and especially provocative way), cock teasing -- when practised as an *art*, in conjunction with an already sexual and loving relationship -- will lead to the whitest-hot sex you've ever had.

I suppose I should give you an example...

OK, there was the time that we were meeting his parents for a New York Philharmonic concert, and we'd just been to a Yankees game... (He'd tried to convince me we should make love in the back of my SUV in the Yankees' parking lot before the game, but I began the tease right there. "No, no, no!" I said playfully, giving him a peck on the cheek as I gave his balls a quick squeeze through his jeans.)

...After the game, as we were heading down a major avenue in Washington Heights (I was driving), I placed my right hand on his left knee, running my manicured red nails over it to give him the shivers. When he let out a soft moan, I moved my hand down to his inner thigh, and made slow circles with my fingers.

I could see he was getting turned on. He opened his legs to give me greater access to his thigh. He closed his eyes, as if overcome by pleasure. And, there was a huge bulge growing between his legs! I thought: *OK, he's all right with this; let's go for the whole thing!*

The bottom line: I just love the shape of his cock, and I love holding it even when we're not making love. I love making it hard, too, and looking at it grow and change color as I play with it. His erection is about 10 inches long, and it's the *widest* one I've ever had the pleasure to know! It's a pretty pinkish red, and it gets redder and redder the longer I tease it.

If I play with it long enough, clear seminal fluid starts to drip from his penis hole, which absolutely drives me wild! His pre-cum, as I call it, is pleasantly salty to the taste; if I hadn't been driving, I'd have been licking it up, because I LOVE it! Once he begins dripping, it's a confirmation to me that I've really got his juices boiling.

Mind you, this was a sunny, warm day, and there were plenty of people walking on the crowded streets of New York City. There were also lots of red lights we'd have to stop at on our long journey to Lincoln Center. So I knew that what I was about to do would be a bit risky, being so out in the open. But, then again, I knew that the public nature of my attack would drive him all the more wild!

I now moved my hand directly above his genitals, and found he was already practically bursting out of his pants. It must have hurt him to have had such a huge hard-on in such tight jeans!

For a few minutes, I traced his outlines -- from his balls all the way up to his sexy penis head, alternately using my nails and my flattened hand to tease and enflame his most sensitive parts: his scrotum, the root of his cock, his shaft, and his cock head.

When I thought I'd aroused him to a sufficient state, I went in for the kill, so to speak, quickly unbuttoning his pants (he was wearing no belt), and unzipping his fly before he could think things through and protest. No, I was too quick and he was too far gone to put up a fight.

Now rubbing him through the thin fabric of his cotton bikini briefs, I knew I'd removed his ability to resist. It was making him crazy.

He couldn't believe I was doing this to him in public! I could tell he was a bit concerned about the location, because he slunk down in his seat and raised his right knee to the dashboard, *as if that really would have given him some privacy!* I don't think so!

Yet, *no one on the crowded streets seemed to notice that I was giving my boyfriend a hand job!*

Knowing he was putty in my hands, that he was subject to my every whim, was tremendously exciting. I was getting wet just imagining what my touch was doing to him.

Now, because *slowness* is a virtue when teasing your man to his hottest state of arousal, I then *patiently* peeled down the elastic of his undies until his swollen, soft pink cock head was exposed, as if this task was in need of savoring. I didn't want to make him come, or get too hot too fast; this was like an achingly slow strip tease...in *reverse*...with *me* firmly in control.

I turned to look. I felt my pussy pulsate upon seeing his lovely head straining, enormously engorged, as if it was trying to get free of his undies. I was, of course, quite hot by now, but I didn't let it show; that's also a necessary part of properly cock teasing your man. (If you sigh, or let him know you're getting excited, he might turn the tables on you, or, at the very least, lose focus on what you're doing to him.)

Leaving him in this state for awhile, I took my thumb and rubbed the small part that's just below the V at the front of his cock head, his frenulum. (I've been told a man's frenulum is like a clit. You can make your man come from rubbing that part by itself, if you do it the right way, with the right touch and rhythm.)

OK, then -- after doing this for awhile -- I moved

my thumb up to the hole at the top of his penis, making a few quick circles there, to pick up as much lubrication from his pre-cum as possible. (If you haven't already noticed it, using lubrication takes a hand job to a higher level.) Then, when I returned my attention to his frenulum, my thumb now slippery wet, covered with his pre-cum, I could tell my use of his lubrication was making him much hotter than before.

Realizing I might make him come if I kept this up too long, I reluctantly (with a sigh), abandoned this ploy in favor of pulling his underwear down entirely. He was no longer in a mode to resist, and, in fact, he obediently helped me pull down his jeans and his briefs, so that his privates were totally exposed for all to see, his pants now down around his ankles. (I *love* putting my man into a state like this -- so *vulnerable*, and *sexy!*)

He was really groaning now, as I tickled his balls. It didn't matter to me whether I was actively driving or if we were at a red light, where people crossing the street were close enough to have seen what I was doing if they had simply turned their heads our way -- I just kept up the onslaught. (Actually, I got the impression that he grew more excited when we were closest to being caught in the act! He knew when we'd come to a stop; his eyes would open, and he'd raise his bare legs in a vain attempt to cover up, putting his knees on the dash.)

We had *tens* of streets to pass before we got anywhere close to where we were heading, Lincoln Center, which was nearly one *hundred* streets away. I had chosen the slowest route possible, to allow me a maximum amount of time for my cock tease. So, my loving torturing went on for at least a half hour, if not more.

Placing the thick bottom part of my palm near the head of his penis while surrounding his bag with my fingers, I did slow circles, nail teasing, everything I could think of, before grabbing his entire shaft for the next round of this cock tease. I had to fight off my urge to hold his cock in this way for quite some time. That's what he so desperately wanted most, so, naturally, in the spirit of the tease, I had to put that off until last.

With my thumb on top of the soft fleshy tube that runs on his cock's underside, and my fingers doing their best to surround the meat of his shaft, I stroked him *silly* -- first with soft, feathery light strokes, and then, as we got closer to our destination, with more insistent motions -- always backing off in tempo and intensity when it seemed like he might be nearing his climax.

It absolutely drove...him...mad!!! I pretended to be surprised when we were within a block or two of the parking garage, suddenly yanking my hand away from him.

"Uh, oh -- you'd better get your pants on, hon; we're almost there!" I said sweetly, with just the right touch of innocence.

"Oh," he groaned, clearly burning up and frustrated.

His cheeks were flushed and he appeared woozy from all the sexual stimulation. I chuckled as he seemed to be having some trouble with coordination as he struggled to pull his undies and pants back on -- I'd sidled up to a parking space and he needed to get himself together, fast, before someone finally did notice that he was half-naked.

I quickly parked the car and left him there on slow burn, telling him I had to get something from the drug store. I could see that he had a small, circular wet spot on the front of his trousers, and I smiled, pleased that I'd accomplished my task.

He'd be feverish for the rest of the evening, through the concert, hungering for me to finish the job...a slave to the cravings that I had ignited. I had sent him into a state of heat, if you will, and he'd feel the need to make love to me when we got home, which is, after all, what I wanted.

But my sweet sexual tormenting of him didn't end there. Throughout the meal with his mom and dad, and the concert, my hand was constantly on his thigh, scandalously high up, fueling his flames. I don't think his hard-on ever went down during the concert, poor thing! (Smile.)

Plus, on the ride home, in the back of his parents' car, I continued to enflame his cock. I even pulled his hard-on out of the top of his briefs, after I'd ever so quietly unbuttoned and unzipped his pants (so that his parents couldn't tell what I was doing). I got the feeling his father suspected something was up, but I had positioned myself so my boyfriend's condition was hidden from his dad's view, so I didn't care! (Actually, the possibility of getting caught was part of the cock tease; it was obviously making my boyfriend hot -- his boner was as big as I'd ever seen it!)

The ride home covered at least 50 miles, and I made it the ride of Joe's life. All the way home, I had his cock in my hand, keeping it rock hard while priming it stay hot enough to come...but not quite.

I'd stroke the top of his shaft with my thumb a half dozen times or more, and then I'd stop, just squeezing it and holding it for awhile. Then, I'd repeat the process. It wasn't long before clear seminal fluid was *pouring* out of his cock. By the time we drew near to Joe's parents' house and I had to put him back in his pants, his belly was practically *covered* in the sticky, sexy ooze.

That night, after his mom and dad had gone to bed and we were alone in their house, I took him into their guest room and stripped him naked. But, even then, I *delayed* what he wanted the most, which was to come. Instead, I continued the wicked cock tease.

Laying him on the bed, I fingered, stroked, licked, sucked, teased, pulled -- I did everything I could think of to his cock EXCEPT make it come. I'd break off the action every time he began to squirm or moan too much, indicating he was nearing his orgasm. I think I teased him a whole *hour* before giving him the hand job I knew would make him blow his top.

And...what's so great about it is...when he did come, he absolutely shot the most cum *I'd ever seen.* And -- get this -- he shot off like a rocket, the farthest I've ever seen. Some of it hit his face, but most of it shot OVER his head and onto the wall!

Afterward, he languished on the bed as if he'd been knocked out. He could barely move. That really pleased me; it meant I'd really gotten him good! He seemed stunned by how overwhelming his orgasm had been, and he stayed in an incapacitated condition for some time.

In fact, I *left* him like that, telling him I'd best be off before his parents busted us. He told me later that -- once he was able to move -- it took him quite awhile to figure out how to get his jism stain off the wall without leaving telltale signs his parents might find! (I could just imagine!)

He's not going to forget what I did to him anytime soon. Plus, here was a great new memory he and I would enjoy recalling for years to come!

I smiled as I left him, pretty sure that in the coming days he'd probably pop a boner thinking about what I'd done to him. Perhaps he'd even need to attend to it, to get some relief.

So, ladies, the message is: don't neglect the power of a masterful cock tease, to keep your man in a constant state of heat, with an urgent desire to be with you. Cock teasing is just another great way to love your man. And, if you knock his socks off, he'll *love* you all the more!

P.J.'s Story: My Full Release Massage

With a flourish, I whipped off my crimson cashmere sweater, gently placing it on the chair beside the massage table, simultaneously slipping my bare feet out of my hot red fuck-me pumps.

My friend Paula had made special arrangements so that I might enjoy a days' worth of pampering at an exclusive spa in Beverly Hills, telling me to be sure and sign up for a massage with someone special (I'll call him Stefan, to protect his real identity).

Paula had given me a smile and a wink when she said

I should tell Stefan that I wanted a "full release" massage. Not knowing what that was, I assumed it was the newest massage therapy in vogue at the time.

From the time I entered the spa, I was over-whelmed by its opulence and the lavish attention I got.

After indicating my desire to take a massage with Stefan, I was escorted through a labyrinth of breathtakingly decorated corridors by the tuxedoed host. He led me to a nicely appointed room, telling me: "Please undress to the level you feel comfortable with, Mrs. C———. Stefan will be with you presently."

I had never had a professional massage before and so I was a bit nervous. It did feel sinfully nice getting undressed. I don't know why.

I felt there was no reason to be shy in front of a massage therapist, so I decided right away to peel off all of my clothes to enable Stefan to make this the most delightful experience possible. I didn't want anything to get in the way of his servicing me.

I should tell you that I was married at the time, but it had been three years since my husband Tom had made love to me. Actually, he'd barely touched me at all during those years (that's why Paula had sent me for the massage).

Unconsciously, I think I was hoping the massage would make up for my body's years of neglect. But, naturally, I realized that was not likely to happen. This was going to be, unfortunately or not, nothing more than a professional encounter with a therapist.

And, of course, that was just fine. I was sure it would leave me feeling less tense, which is what I needed. Yet, I found myself removing my wedding band and hiding it in my purse, convincing myself that I was doing so to make it easier for Stefan to massage that hand.

Whipping off my red cashmere sweater, I placed it carefully over the back of the chair that was in the corner of the room.

Undoing the hooks of my black lace bra with one hand, I slipped the cups away from my nicely shaped medium-sized still-uplifted breasts (which belied my 38 years and happily continued to turn the eyes of men *and* women), and deposited my bra over my sweater.

A quick glance in the mirror by the table made me smile. I was pleased to see that I still had "it."

My nipples grew hard and a sexy feeling over-

took my body – from my face down – tickling me
like a wave in the warm Caribbean sea, as the
naughtiness of walking around bare-breasted
registered in my brain.

Realizing Stefan would be entering the room in
minutes, I hastily pulled off my panty hose and
panties, placing them on the seat of the chair. I
then unzipped my short black skirt, laying it down
above my panties.

Buck naked, I grabbed the small wisp of a towel
that was on top of the massage table, and, laying
down on my stomach, I was arranging it as best I
could over my backside, but it didn't cover very
much and...the door was opening!

I felt a rush of heat on my cheeks as I saw
Stefan for the first time, as he entered the room.
He was *stunning*.

He was "cut" – his arms were bulging with
muscles, his pecks straining to burst out from his
tight-fitting white T-shirt. I surmised he was in his
late 20s.

I had almost forgotten that I hadn't quite finished
adjusting my towel, but, with a reassuring smile,
Stefan noticed my plight and strode right over,
turning the towel sideways. The entire length of
the backs of my legs, however, were still exposed.

As he slid it just a ways *above* the crease of my bottom; a shiver raced through my body.

"Here," he said, "that's better!"

The dulcet sound of his voice seemed to vibrate through my whole body, and caused some kind of tickle in my neck. It felt as if some of the organs inside my body had released chemicals, heightening my sensitivity.

Remembering what my friend had instructed me to tell Stefan, I blurted out: "Paula said I should ask for a full-release massage," managing to conquer a sudden shyness that had crept over me.

Stopping for a split second, he said: "Really?"

I felt a bit sexy and ashamed at the same time, for which my inner voice scolded me. *People get massages every day,* I heard the voice tell me. *There's nothing to be ashamed of!*

I now felt Stefan's hands upon me, doing what felt like feather-light caresses across the backs of my thighs. His handiwork gave me a sensuous tingle that I hadn't felt in quite awhile, and it didn't take long before I realized that his delicious hand strokes were causing a moistness between my legs.

Oh no, I thought. *I'm getting wet! I hope he doesn't notice!* (Of course, how could he? But we all suspect that men can somehow *sense* when we're wet, don't we?)

I could feel drops trickling down my vagina. I was praying he'd stop before they dripped down my labia, where they could indeed be seen. But he kept up the sensuous feather stroking, the stroking that was steadily getting me damper

"Oh!" I heard myself say, in a breathy way. It was involuntary; I couldn't help myself. I was a bit embarrassed by letting out a moan, but he was playing my body like an instrument, and I was feeling as if I was putty in his hands, without strength now to protest whatever he might do.

I felt him next gently spreading my inner thighs with both of his hands, moving the towel to expose my entire bottom. With that, the walls of my vagina involuntarily quivered.

Oh God! I thought. *This is not what I thought would happen!*

I wondered whether I should stop Stefan right there. He was making me hot, and I wasn't totally comfortable with that.

But, as he moved his hands up my thighs, I realized I could no longer find the strength to protest. I *wanted* him to touch me there – and higher up, too!

It felt like his right thumb had oh so softly touched my labia, like a light brush stroke, but I wasn't sure if I was imagining things. It could have simply been his breath tickling me down there. It was awfully light, whatever it was I had felt.

But, no, there it was again. Did he do it by accident or was he teasing me?

It sounds really bad on my part, but I honestly arrived at the point that I didn't care, really. I now wanted him to go further.

I let go a sigh, and wiggled my bottom a little, hoping it would invite him to explore my inner recesses.

"How does it feel?" he inquired.

"Oh…" I purred, "it feels just *great!*"

"That's good," he replied.

"Paula had said you were great at full-release massage," I added, "and I can see why!"

He stopped momentarily, and I wasn't sure why. Maybe he was gauging my response, or maybe he was experiencing some of the sexual heat that was now burning me up.

Moving again, I felt his big warm hands surrounding my buttocks, lasciviously rotating them in a way that only fanned the flames that were overtaking me. He was separating the globes, his palms also acting to open and close my pussy lips, which were now really tingling.

(*Was he suppose to manipulate my pussy lips in this way, however indirectly?*, I wondered briefly. But then I convinced myself that it was totally innocent.)

"Oh!" I said, in a half-whisper.

As I heard my own voice, I realized instantly that it was an admission to Stefan that I was aroused, and, perhaps, that I was throwing caution to the wind and inviting him to go beyond the normal realm of things.

His open hands now moved slightly lower toward the backs of thighs, his motions indirectly serving to rhythmically open and close my labia, which I could feel were now swollen and wet.

And then he did it. This was unmistakable.

I felt his thumb and forefinger on my clit, but, I could not bring myself to resist his sexual advances. Part of me wanted to, but part of me -- the stronger part -- wanted him to continue.

"Oh," I said, groaning a bit too loudly to be mistaken for anything but encouragement for Stefan to continue.

I raised my shoulders and eyebrows, in fact, in an apologetic gesture, looking back at Stefan, indicating I knew that I should be more quiet. He put his right index finger across his smiling mouth, in a silent "shhh!" gesture.

I shook my head *yes*. I didn't want anyone interrupting this!

The next thing I knew, Stefan was lowering the table with a turn of a knob, and, pulling my hips toward him with both hands, I felt my bare feet touch the marble floor as I was now half-standing. I heard him unknotting his sweatpants and then I looked back to see him pushing his pants and undies down to his ankles.

Reaching over for some lotion and deftly rubbing it all over my loins, back and forth, back and forth, he furtively slipped his middle finger into my now-aching cunt. Making ever wider circles, my hips wiggling in response, my libido now driving me crazy with desire.

Removing his finger, I felt Stefan placing the head of his cock against my pussy lips, sliding it in just a centimeter or two, before pulling out again entirely. Every time he entered me, he'd push it in a little farther. The evident tease was making me impatient for him to fill me up completely.

"Oh, God!" I shouted, accidentally, realizing that it might have been heard through the walls, which were probably paper thin.

I'd been trying to keep my voice to a whisper, or, better yet, stay entirely silent. But it had become too much. I wanted all of him. Now!

Reaching back with both hands, I grabbed the bottom of his muscular thighs and pulled him toward me, melting away as I drew the entire length of his hard-on into my vagina. I felt my vaginal walls stretching as he plunged further and further in, until I felt as if I was going to come.

Holding my hips firmly against his with both of his hands, he then began a vigorous rocking motion, in and out a couple of inches at a time, over and over. I closed my eyes as intense pleasure swept through my body, from my pussy right up to my head. I then felt his right hand, moving over my belly and then down to my clit, as he began to kiss the back of my neck, driving me wilder and wilder.

I remember worrying a little about the squeaking of the table as he continued to pound away at my cunt, but I didn't stop him; it was just as I liked it!

I did fleetingly wonder what anyone who might have heard the noise might have thought. But that was only a passing thought; primarily what I was thinking was, *wow, this guy is fucking my eyeballs out!*

So, when there was a knock on the door, my worst fears came true!

But, without missing a beat, Stefan averted disaster. Holding steady for a moment, he called out: "I'm doing a massage!"

"Oh, sorry!" came the masculine reply, and, with that, Stefan immediately renewed his efforts.

After five or ten more minutes, I heard myself – against my better judgment – tell him I wanted him to come inside me. Reaching out to hold his balls with my left hand while pulling his body tightly against mine with my right, I heard Stefan let out an audible groan.

I desperately wanted to feel his cock throbbing in me, during the height of his orgasm. Rubbing his balls seemed to hasten the inevitable, and then it happened.

He began ramming me faster and faster, until I felt his cock gushing inside me, the faster pace of his insertions sending me over the top at the same time.

"Yes!" I blurted out, again, by mistake, unable to keep totally quiet.

All Stefan could do was stand there, a bit hunched over, breathing heavily, unable to move due to the aftereffects of his orgasm.

My vagina was quivering for what seemed like minutes afterward. I clung to the soft tabletop, catching my breath.

True to form, I immediately began to feel a little guilty about this affair, even before the delirium from my orgasm had worn off. And I began to wonder whether Stefan had provided this service to all of his female clientele.

"I guess you've done this before, but I'm a little ashamed of myself," I said, getting off the table to find my clothes and cover up.

"Well...no, actually," he answered, with some hesitation...and some confusion.

A look of sudden horror overtook Stefan's face, and he hastily pulled his pants up.

"Oh I...I've made a big mistake! I'm *really* sorry!" he said.

I gathered at first that he thought I was going to complain and get him fired. But, apparently something else was at work here.

Looking at me earnestly, as if he had to explain something of complexity and sensitivity, he whispered:

"Paula had told me you were anxious to meet me, and that this would be a great way to spend our first date," he explained, growing more and more nervous. "And she said if you asked me for a 'full-release massage' that I was to understand that you wanted me to make love to you. I thought you knew Paula was sort of setting us up."

It seemed as if Paula had played a joke on both of us (I could have killed her when I put two and two together). Everything worked out all right, but things might have turned seriously nasty if Stefan hadn't filled me in on the details, and made everything clear to me.

And I couldn't fault Stefan totally for what had developed. In retrospect, I realized that I might have been more responsible for what had happened than he.

Didn't I did tell him, twice, that I wanted a "full release" massage? Although I didn't know it at the time, I found out later that a "full release" massage was an industry term for a massage that included a sexual encounter. Unaware, I had literally *asked* him to fuck me, and I'm sure it had sounded to Stefan that I was very clear about what I wanted him to do to me.

(That's undoubtedly why he hesitated each time I made that request, and why he waited until after the *second* time I had requested it to actually comply with my stated wishes. He was trying to see if I really meant what I had said, and, finally, he determined, however wrongly, that I had.)

So I was, needless to say, at least *partly* to blame for Stefan's confusion.

Long story short -- my sixth sense, which had told me everything was OK during my first experience with Stefan, also made me ask him for his phone number afterward.

So, Stefan and I began to see each other following our sexy first encounter and, upon getting to know him better, I realized early on that he was everything that I had sought in a man. Our first "date" admittedly was unorthodox, but I have no regrets; it proved to be the start of something wonderful.

Had my husband performed his husbandly duties, I would never dreamed of straying. But he hadn't.

So, that led to my being vulnerable and needy, which led to my weakness, which led to Stefan, which led to a fabulous new life, full of the love that I had craved for so long.

J.B.'s Story: Touch Me In The Morning

It's always difficult for me in the morning to wake up beside Paul without touching him.

Paul's got one of those bodies that makes you want to come just *looking* at it. It's especially hard to restrain myself in the morning because he sleeps in the nude and invariably wakes up with a delicious hard-on (and his penis is...a *pretty* penis, one that you want to surround with your lips).

Plus, he's the best *lover* I've ever had. He really knows how to curl my toes!

He's the most creative lover I've ever had, and he's got one of those non-stop cocks. He

can go on forever, until I'm senseless from all the pleasure!) Yep, since meeting Paul, I've been sooo horny. All day, every day, I want him inside me.

What's really tough is that I think about him every second at *work* (it gets pretty hard for me to concentrate on what I'm supposed to be doing). To my embarrassment, my ruminations result in my panties getting wet while I'm on the job.

So, I have trouble keeping my hands off of him. Like the other day: I was already a bit late for work, but I'd been awake most of the night hungering for his attention because his cock was hard from the time we went to bed to the time I woke up.

I like pressing my body against his under the covers, and I can usually get an occasional rise out of him while he's asleep, but this night, his erection wouldn't quit! And, naturally, with his hard-on resting against my back all night long, I was hot and wet...*all night long*. I didn't want to awaken him, though; I knew he needed the sleep.

However, once the clock turned 6, I thought ...*now he's fair game*. Slowly easing my right hand down to his tummy, I found the head of his cock and gently began stroking it. I thought I provoked a soft moan from him, but I wasn't sure.

So I took my thumb and started softly rubbing the ridge at the top of his shaft (which I've been told is called the frenulum; it's supposed to be the most sensitive part of a man's penis).

Feeling my nipples grow taut as a flush warmed my face and chest, I could see Paul was being responsive if not *receptive* to my advances. His hips were beginning to move sympathetically and his moans were now clearly audible.

So, I decided, *what the hey*, and proceeded to denude Paul of his bedsheets. Exposing his beautiful, slender body to the morning sunlight peeking into the bedroom through the shades only made me want him more.

His cock was rampantly standing up, and it was *breathtaking*. The muscles in his chest and arms tensed and, in doing so, they hardened, making me lose my breath momentarily.

One thing I love about Paul is how strong he is. I've never had a man before who had the combination of brute strength and sexual staying power that Paul has, and I couldn't wait to tease him into such a state of passion that he would have no choice but to enter me. I desperately needed to quench the fires that were now burning out of control inside my body.

Reaching over to my left to the olive oil I keep on my nightstand (olive oil is a great sex tool), I anointed Paul's nice erection with the lubricant, vigorously masturbating him with my right hand, while cuddling his balls with my left.

"You are soooo big, Paul!" I said, as his groans grew louder.

"Do you want to be inside me?" I asked, but he seemed lost in the moment. So, I resorted to shouting: "I want you inside me...NOW!"

Opening his eyes suddenly, Paul laughed at my comical heavy-handedness.

"OK, baby," he said. "You know I wouldn't deny you my love."

Rolling onto his side, Paul then directed his stiff member so it was resting -- sideways -- on the lips of my dripping cunt. Then, ever so slowly, he slid it in, one inch at a time.

Holding both of my legs up off the bed with his right arm, he began a slow fucking motion, perhaps to loosen up my tight twat. But, I was so wound up, I *came* shortly after he started caressing my thighs with his left hand.

The touch of his hand on the backs of my legs was like a spark to a gas leak, and I could feel my juices filling my cunt with the onset of my orgasm.

"Ooohh, Paul!" I exclaimed, the orgasm knocking the wind out of me. "Oh, man!"

Wasting no time, he then put me in a position he'd never had me in before, which got me excited all over again. Putting my feet over his shoulders now, while sitting up on his splayed knees, he directed his hugely swollen cock toward my steaming hot pussy.

Rubbing my crack up and down with the head of his cock, he must have realized by its wetness that I was more than ready for him. Before I knew it, he'd slipped his long shaft into me, making me gasp for air. I felt as if my *soul* was on fire.

Sensing how hot I was, I'm sure Paul realized there was no need for the usual slow dance of foreplay, so he immediately began deep-thrusting the shit out of me. Now holding my feet up in the air in his powerful left hand, Paul made me feel very vulnerable, in a sexy way.

Letting out yelps of "oh" and "ah," my heart pounding, breathing quickly and deeply now, my pussy juices were now coming down in a veritable *flood*. My eyes opening wide with every thrust of Paul's hips, my body tensing, I knew I was close to the brink of coming again.

"Oh, yes, *yes*, *go* Paul!" I said, urging him on as

he now went *wild* inside my pussy, dicking the shit out of me.

And then he did something else he'd never done before, which sent me over the top...As my ear-piercing cries announced the start of a tidal wave-sized orgasm, he took one of my big toes in his mouth and sucked on it furiously, making my orgasm explode into a body-length seizure that absolutely ripped my head off (or so it felt).

"You like getting your toes sucked, don't you?" he said in a sexy bedroom voice, obviously proud of what he'd done.

"Yes, baby," I whispered.

"Good," he replied.

...And so he did it again, sucking my other big toe this time, as his merciless pounding tore up my pussy, sending me into another nuclear-scale orgasm. My head was reeling, but he wasn't about to stop.

Changing positions now -- lowering my legs and placing them between his -- he leaned over to cover my heaving body with his hot, sweaty torso. Looking at me with a boyish smile, he put his arms around my back and embraced me, his hard cock completely filling my pussy.

Slowly lowering his face to mine, he took his big,

hot tongue, and provocatively laved my mouth from one corner to the other, as if he were licking my *pussy*. I don't know if you'll believe this, but, in the heat of the moment, the feeling of being impaled on his hard-on gave me deep sensations inside my cunt that grew and grew, until they made me *come* again!

"Oh baby, oh baby," I groaned from the wonderful agony of it, squirming under Paul's muscular body.

"Mmmm," Paul remarked, clearly enjoying my state of excitement.

Kissing me urgently now, I remember thinking how sexy it was kissing Paul while his rock solid cock was buried so deeply inside of me.

And then he got an impish grin.

"Now," he said, taking my right hand and placing it above my clit, "I want you to show me what you did to yourself before we met, when you were dreaming of having a big cock like mine inside your pussy."

"You want me to...masturbate?" I asked tentatively, a bit shy about doing that.

"Work your clit over, baby," he urged, his thick, deep voice sounding every bit as sexy as Barry White's. "Make it come."

I'd never done myself for a man before, but I love Paul so much I didn't think twice about doing what he wished. Actually, I was surprised at how *natural* it seemed, and *thrilling*, as I obediently began making circles around my clit with my index and middle fingers.

"Oh!" I moaned. "Oh, Paul..." The idea of doing myself in front of my boyfriend -- with his hard-on still straight up my cunt -- made me so hot, I was already dying to come again.

"That's right, baby," he encouraged, as his newly-begun pelvic thrusting loosened up my defenses.

"Rub it good, honey. I know you want to come. Feel my cock and show me what it makes you want to do."

"Yes, yes," I panted, his words melting away any remaining shyness I might have had. All I knew now was a sense of overwhelming desire -- the desire for satisfaction.

"Do it, baby," he continued in soft bass tones. "Do it good. I want to hear you scream."

Scream I did. Losing total control, his voice and cock whipping me into such a state that I couldn't WAIT to get release, I attacked my clitoris with a fury that I brought down a *tidal wave* of cum juices as I was engulfed in head-to-toe shock waves of excitement, of incredible orgasmic intensity.

And with that, uncontrollable passion overtook me, making me its slave. Moving involuntarily, as it seemed, I hungrily pulled Paul's buttocks hard against my body, while leaning up to suck on one of his nipples, hard.

"Oh, you're going to make me come!" he said, as if he was incredulous about what I was doing to him, inside.

"Yes, baby, come for me," I said, never letting his nipple slip out of the grasp of my lips. Man, I was sucking and licking the *shit* out of it.

His in-and-out rocking motion grew faster and faster as he became more excited. I could feel his cock grow bigger and bigger as he reached his boiling point after just a few minutes.

Pulling his cock out quickly, Paul took himself by the shaft and rubbed his burning hot hard-on on my belly until I could feel it throbbing as it squirted its hot jism onto my skin.

Screaming "oh...shhhhit!," Paul then threw himself on top of me in a state of rapturous exhaustion.

Listening to him breathing heavily, it suddenly

dawned on me how late I was for work, but, somehow, I didn't seem to *care*.

Actually, I found it hard just to physically get up. I would have preferred to have stayed in bed all day long, making love to Paul. Lately, that's all I have wanted to do.

"I'm going to be thinking of you all day long," I whispered, as I peeled myself away from Paul and padded toward the shower (walking with some difficulty).

As I stood outside the shower, my hand feeling the water flow to test the temperature, I felt two hands on my hips.

"Love ya baby," Paul whispered in my ear, his warm cheek nuzzling my neck.

Turning around, I gave him a great big hug and a passionate, wet kiss. Feeling his warm, bare skin against my body, the warm water showering over us, felt so...*fulfilling*. I didn't want to break the embrace.

"Love ya right back," I said, putting my head on his shoulder.

I remember thinking: *this* is what makes life so worthwhile.

G.V.'s Story: I Like To Watch

People are so different when they're making love, don't you think? I've always been fascinated by this. I mean, what a man looks like with his clothes off (and his hard-ON) is just part of the picture. There are still two parts left to the mystery, aren't there?

No matter what he looks like, fully-attired or bare, there is still the question of how good a *cocksman* he is. In other words, does he know how to use what he has? And lastly, what kind of lover is he?

Actually, the answer to the last question is sometimes, to me, a make-it or break-it proposition. Is he creative?

Will you get bored, or will he constantly surprise and excite you? And, is he a square, or is he willing to do whatever you want him to do?

You'll never know the answers to these questions until you get him home and let him do his stuff.

Personally, I want a man who is sometimes dominant, and sometimes submissive.

For instance, take Stu, my boyfriend. While he's in his 40s, he's got the body of an athletic 30-year old. I didn't realize how really hot his body was until I first undressed him. But that was just one of a host of welcome revelations I experienced.

Looking at him, you'd never know he was such a great lover. He's very handsome (with a face that's real easy on the eyes), but he has a boy-next-door kind of wholesomeness, too (which belies the animal he becomes when he's behind closed doors). So, I was a bit apprehensive when we first met; I wasn't sure he'd meet my needs as a woman with a voracious sex drive.

Until I got this mild-mannered man in bed, I didn't realize how *great* he was in the saddle, always ready to take control and drive me wild, with a bag of tricks that might make Casanova green with envy.

But, not only that -- I was pleased to find that he was also very *compliant* when I'd ask him to do something special for me. That's also something I want in a man!

I want to be able sometimes to take the upper hand and tell him what to do. Like masturbate.

I can't speak for all women, but, c'mon girls, don't we like to watch? Don't we get hot seeing our man take things into his own hands? LOL (laughing out loud).

For example, the other morning, Stu and I were lying in bed, and I was teasing him, telling him he should become a gigolo and service rich women, because he has the talent and the body for it. (I was only kidding, of course. I'm too attached to Stu. I'd die if he were with another woman!)

Anyway, the point is, I was only teasing Stu to see if I could get a rise out of him (both literally and figuratively), and to see what he'd say.

As I playfully discussed how he might do as a gigolo, I felt his cock grow really hard (we were spooning, naked, and his cock was pressing against my butt).

Stu just laughed when I suggested he could charge $1,000 a night for his services -- but that would be his base fee, only for performing in the missionary position. Anything other requests, I told him, would cost more.

"...Like if she wanted you to give her head, or masturbate for her," I said, turning my body around so I could finger Stu's balls.

"Do women like to watch men masturbate?" he asked, in between groans brought on by my attention to his balls.

"They sure do," I answered.

"Well, I've never been asked to," he replied.

"You just *were*, but you didn't realize it!" I said, smiling broadly.

Looking at me for a second, as if to see if I was serious, Stu responded:

"I'll masturbate for you, if you want me to. Just let me know when."

"How 'bout now?" I said, squeezing the head of his cock.

He smiled at me as if to say *"you're really kinky, aren't you?!"* But then he followed through on my request.

Turning his body around 180 degrees, so that his feet were resting on top of the bed's headboard and his cock was inches from my face, Stu's left hand found its way down to his rampant hard-on, where he started to tickle his balls with his fingers, and rub his shaft and cock head with the meat of his palm.

"That's a nice position," I said in my sexiest voice, flashing a smile of encouragement.

As he dutifully started doing himself, I began to suck one of his nipples while I teased the other into hardness with the fingers of my right hand. (I admit it; my sexual tastes are a bit on the edge. I LOVE playing with my man's nipples! I love feeling them get hard as I suck them, or watch them grow hard as I tickle them with my fingers!)

All the while, however, I was looking down at his busy hand, not wanting to miss a thing!

I immediately noticed, for instance, that his penis was more swollen and red than I'd ever seen it. In fact, it was positively HUGE! (By the look of it, I thought: *he's really getting off on masturbating for me.*)

"Is that how large you get when you're inside me?" I whispered?

"Yes," he whispered back.

"Is that how you usually do yourself?" I asked, as he took his shaft in his fist and began to jerk himself off.

"Sometimes," he answered, "but I usually look at something, while I'm doing it."

"Like what?"

"Like some old Playboys I have lying around."

"WHERE are they?" I pleaded, anxious to see him jerk off at the sight of naked women in a men's magazine.

"In my top drawer, over there," he said, pointing in the drawer's direction.

Jumping out of bed, I rummaged through his stash of masturbation aids.

"Oh, there's a video here, too!" I said, but Stu didn't respond. He was beginning to get real excited, sometimes lifting his nice bottom off the bed (his feet still on top of the headboard), as his arousal grew.

Grabbing one of the Playboys, I raced back to bed, and asked him to show me which girls he liked the best. (It was an ANCIENT copy -- more than 20 years old. He told me later a friend had given it to him when he was in college. But the women were still attractive to Stu, judging from the way he turned his head to take in the photos.)

I opened the magazine to a random place in the middle, to a spread dedicated to the "Girls of Las Vegas."

"Do you like this one?" I asked him, pointing toward a busty blonde who was pouting on her bed, stark naked, looking as if she was about to do herself. (How do those women pose so naturally, in the nude? I couldn't do it!)

"No," he said. Pointing to a woman who was photographed from behind, standing in silver, strappy mules, smiling into the camera lens as if she were watching the viewer masturbate, he said: "That's the one I like on this page. I love her legs and her behind, and her sweet smile."

He kept masturbating as I turned the pages. When I'd arrived at a page with an erotic story, accompanied by a drawing of a man having sex with a woman, Stu said: "I also like this one," referring to the drawing, in which the woman's legs were crossed behind the man's back, her eyes closed, her feet locked together above his muscular butt. It looked as if the man was really giving it to her.

"Show me who else you like!" I demanded, as my pussy's increasing heat and wetness began to drive me insane.

Stu obediently took his hand off his taut member to point out several of his favorites. They surprised me in that they were nontraditional beauties.

None were very buxom (they certainly did not display the silicon-inflated breasts you see in today's magazines). And all looked like the cute girl next door; none of them went over the top in the way of cheap sexiness.

Stu explained that he liked the ones that looked like they enjoyed being women. He was turned on by the ones who looked like they were having fun and might be fun to be with.

Another favorite photo of his was that of a cute brunette, perching herself upon a pole at a dock, her pretty feet drawn up behind her, one of which sported an ankle bracelet. Her breasts were perky, but on the small side.

"She has big areolas, like you," he explained. "I love big areolas!"

Noticing that he had momentarily stopped masturbating, I motioned with my head that he should get on with it, placing the magazine down next to him so he could focus his fantasies on the brunette. Compliantly lying down again, his cock in his hand, he stared at the bare beauty as I had instructed, until he could no longer keep his eyes open anymore. He was transported, in rapture, and was beginning to moan as his left hand throttled his cock harder and harder...

But I decided at that point that I could take no more. I was burning up from the heat that had built up in me. I know women aren't supposed to be turned on visually, but I most definitely am!

Looking at Stu's stiffie get redder and redder and bigger and bigger had *really* gotten me going. (His dick looked like it was positively going to *burst*. Plus, a steady stream of thick, clear seminal fluid was tantalizingly oozing deliciously from the hole in his cock, and I needed to *taste* it!)

Leaning past Stu's right hip, I gently took control away from him. Taking his stiff cock in both of my hands, I hungrily brought my mouth down to it and tongued the head of his cock, to drink down some of that delicious, salty, sexy fluid. And then I put his gorgeous, rock-hard cock in my mouth.

(I'm very oral. When I get excited, I want to suck *all* of Stu's sexy body parts!)

As I threw myself into the blow job, I noticed Stu, by his reactions, was responding by getting hotter. His feet were pushing up off the headboard lifting his bottom off the bed, and his back was arched, as if he was primed to explode.

With my own excitement level rising, I grew eager to bring him off. Cupping his balls with my right hand while grabbing his shaft with my left, I began to stroke his shaft up and down like I'd seen him doing to himself. I was twisting my left hand slightly as I jerked him off, and my mouth was furiously gobbling down as much as I could of his long, wide cock.

Moaning louder now, I could feel his cock growing even bigger in my mouth. I could make him come any time I wanted now. I decided to go ahead and pull out all of the stops.

I wetted my middle finger with some of my saliva. I then moved it down to the crack of his bottom and began to tease him down there, using the saliva to lubricate his hole.

That really seemed to get him excited! With every flick of my finger, he groaned real loudly.

I kept this up for a minute or two before he was bucking his hips up and down.

"Oh, you're going to do it!" he announced, as if he was a helpless but willing "victim" of my sexual assault. "You're going to make me come!"

And, in seconds, he shot a huge load in my mouth. Sucking harder than before, my head bouncing faster up and down Stu's throbbing penis, I hungrily swallowed every drop that shot out from it. I couldn't get enough!

"Oh! OH! OH!" he shouted, as his cock squirted and squirted, until he could come no more. Pushing my head gently away, Stu begged me to stop: "It's too much, baby, too much!"

Collapsing into a sexy fetal position, his head in my lap, I cuddled with Stu until he had recovered from what I had done to him.

Not long afterward, he was up and ready again, and he gave me the fucking of my life, telling me over and over again how hot I'd made him before, making him masturbate for me.

So, girls, the message is: don't be afraid to boss your man around a bit in bed, or make him jerk off for you! He'll readily comply. And, by the way -- this is a great way to get your man real big before he enters you! After that morning, I've frequently asked Stu to rough himself up for me before we have sex, so I get the maximum bang for my buck, if you don't mind my saying so!

Believe me, you're missing out if you're too shy to tell him what you like. It's REAL hot watching your man masturbate!

Coming Soon from Mystic Ridge Books:

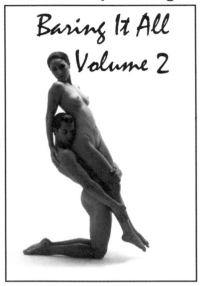

Baring It All
Volume 2

And YOU can be part of it!
If you are a woman who would like to share
(anonymously) an extraordinary love-making
experience in *Baring It All: Volume 2*, send us
your story for consideration, preferably with your
name, address and phone info, to:
Mystic Ridge Books
P.O. Box 66930
Albuquerque, NM 87193
It's a very sexy thing to do! All contact info will
be kept confidential but is needed during editing.
Stories should be steamy, but also tender, loving
and romantic. Permission to use your story freely is
implicit. If your story is chosen, we will send you
the book, free! (For those 21 and older only.)